Dedicated with love to our parents; and especially to the memory of

David Hicks, who would have been so proud if he had lived to see it.

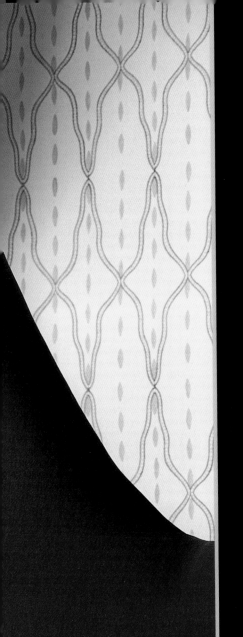

ashley & allegra hicks
DESIGN ALCHEMY

special photography by bill batten
text by ashley hicks

conran
OCTOPUS

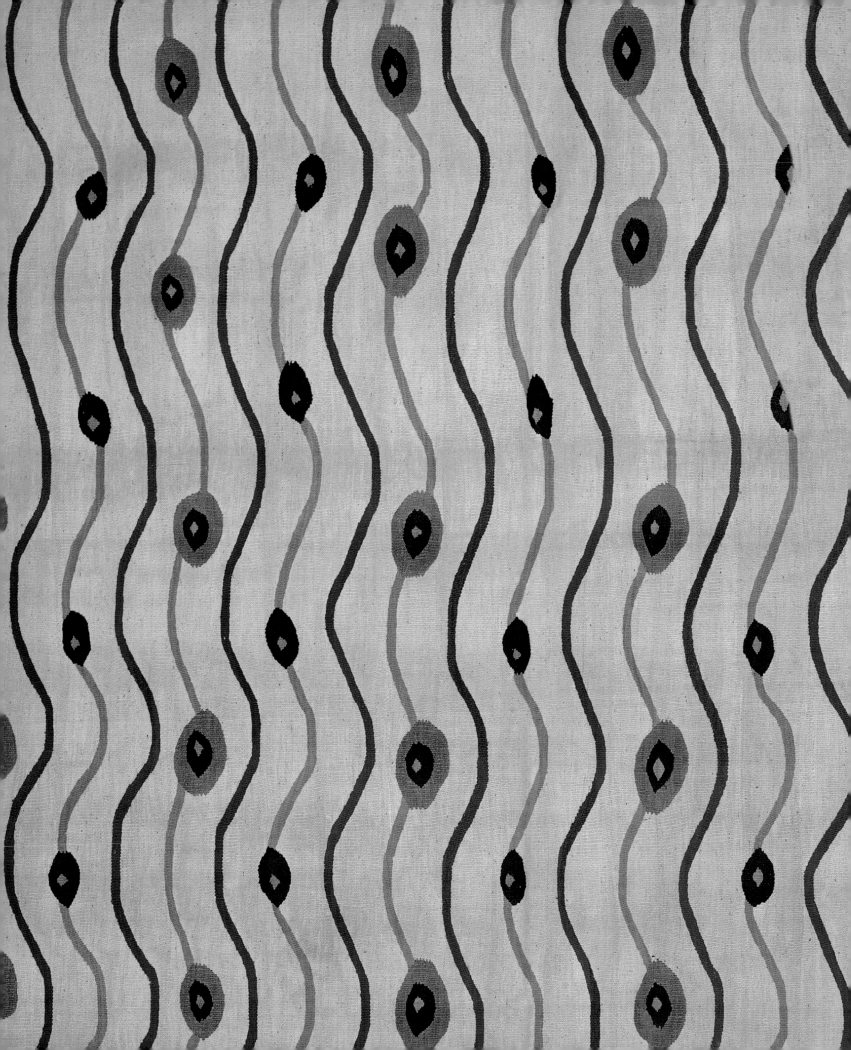

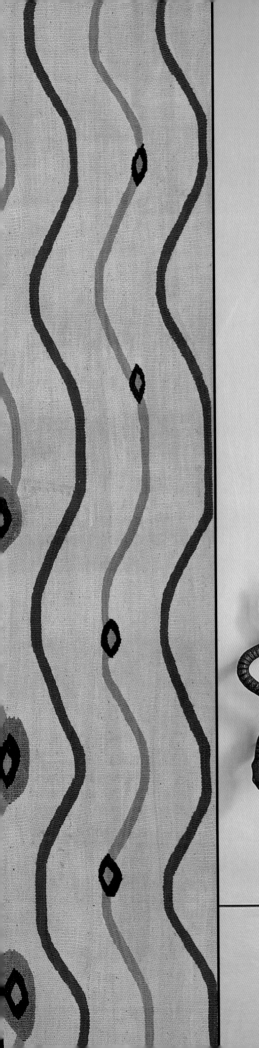

contents

foreword by jeremy irons

I have long been interested in the world of design and decoration. In another life I should have liked to be an architect. For the past two years I have been restoring a medieval keep in south-west Ireland. A great challenge and privilege, and a wonderful contrast to my ephemeral life in films.

When Ashley and Allegra Hicks told me they wanted to create a room for me at the House and Garden Fair 2000, I was delighted. I had met Allegra shortly before and was very impressed by her style and imagination, and was curious to see what she would produce.

The resulting "Dressing Room" was chic and luxurious, but with a simplicity that was very much in tune with my own taste. Like the Hickses, I love India, and share their pleasure in visiting the sub-continent, buying the beautiful old fabrics, furniture and objects that are to be found there.

Indeed, the room they created for me was dominated by a huge, antique Indian architechtural drawing.

This book is a testament to an obsession with design and decoration. The designers show their own work, following a sequence of historical interiors, which range from ancient Pompeii to 1960s England. All of these share an idiosyncrasy, a liveliness, and an interest in the obscure that is refreshingly free of the curse of "good taste".

Our dressing room for Jeremy Irons mixed elements such as my Trellis étagère and a desk, both in exotic Zebrano wood, with my Klismos chair, a wardrobe with doors covered in a Chinese patchwork of Allegra's silks, and a day bed in limed English oak with a mattress covered in Allegra's 'Moon' print.

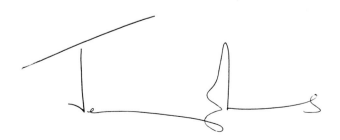

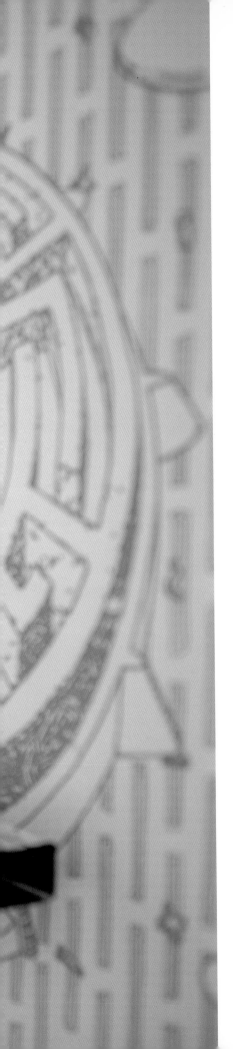

introduction

This book is about that oldest and most fundamental of creative acts, the making of homes. It is also about the partnership between an Italian woman and an English man – my wife and myself – and our work in creating interiors and products to place within them. It is not a thesis or a guide, nor does it provide instructions for 'how to do it'. It simply shows our ideas, our creative processes and their results, and what we have found to be successful solutions to some of the problem interiors we have worked on. Allegra and I rarely design as a team. She designs patterns, rugs, fabrics: soft things. I design architectural interiors and furniture: the hard elements. These skills are combined in many projects, and together we edit our designs, collaborating on ideas, colours and the choice of outside elements.

A wallpaper that Allegra and I designed together includes a maze and an emblem for 'Solution', discovered in a volume of alchemical engravings.

Allegra and I arrived at our current roles by very different routes which included some similar elements: we shared a love of art history and the decorative arts, had many friends in the contemporary art world, and came from backgrounds where design was important, although not in the same way.

Allegra was born and raised in Turin, where her parents were devout modernists with a passion for new design typical of post-war Italy. Her home was a modern steel and glass house filled with the newest in Italian contemporary furniture and lighting, including the famous 1960s Gufram range of jokey polystyrene furniture produced by her father. It was an environment of great modernity and an excitement for the new.

Allegra trained as a graphic designer and fine artist, initially working as a *trompe l'oeil* and fresco painter. This gives her work a painterly, two-dimensional quality, with great strengths in colour and pattern. For several years she produced large-scale paintings, working directly on walls and building up an image in a disciplined, methodical manner. This gives a sense of process and application that is perfectly suited to the kind of design work Allegra has moved into.

I grew up in the English countryside where my father, interior designer David Hicks, had taken a country house and decorated it in a variety of styles that shared a perfectionism and an obsession with detail and history. He made our home into one of the world's most photographed houses, publishing a series of books between 1966 and 1973 that established his style as an international icon of the time. Living in the environment he created was a little unreal at times. He would leave museum-quality objects in 'tablescapes' in the rooms: Aztec gold discs, eighteenth-century rock crystal snuffboxes, or Chinese jade saucers filled with gold dust.

After four years at art school, I trained as an architect, and had a small practice before gradually moving into interior and then furniture design. I was always fascinated by the planning of houses, the division of space and the choice of furniture; my first projects featured intricate built-in furniture, very architectural in character, from which I progressed towards designing a collection. At the same time, Allegra and I started to work together on commissions for interiors, and I gave up my architectural practice to concentrate on this.

The fact that neither of us trained specifically for what we are now doing seems to give us a useful distance. Not having backgrounds in furniture or textile design has meant that we have had to invent our own techniques, and train ourselves through

making things, rather than through theory. It has been similar to an old-fashioned apprenticeship. We have developed designs and techniques, with the manufacturing process informing the design of our products.

Allegra and I look at things in very different ways, and this is reflected in our drawing styles. We each have a different 'eye' and absorb different aspects of the things we see. I am more interested in linear design, in architectural forms and spaces, and in a historical narrative, while Allegra sees more of the atmosphere, colours, the general 'look' of places, and patterns and forms of two dimensions.

This book is the product of both those sets of eyes. It sets forth our inspiration, our design process, and some of our finished projects. It attempts to examine what inspires us, why we have made certain decisions and what has led us to certain paths, without, I hope, becoming pretentious about a subject that could hardly be more mundane and ordinary: the making of homes.

Looking down the stairs of our London house, with a photograph by Federica Tondato on the 1940s French shagreen desk and another by Ingrid Dinter on the wall. The green glass window was in the house when we found it; the small chandelier is by André Dubreuil.

inspired by the classic

This chapter contains a small selection of historical interiors. It is a disparate yet personal collection, united by a common thread of inspiration. Each interior featured here has been, indirectly, a source of inspiration to us in our work; just as each was itself inspired in turn by some earlier source. The inspiration of the past has always been (and will remain) one of the strongest formative influences on any creative endeavour.

However much people may yearn for originality and spontaneity in design, it is impossible to create in a vacuum.

Beneath the dome of his museum in London, Sir John Soane surveys his collection of antique fragments, both stone originals and plaster casts made for him. The training of his architecture students involved study of these fragments and other sources, such as the Athenian hydria, left.

The past is always present – whether as something to react against or to build upon – in everything we make and do.

The interiors we have chosen here vary greatly in scale and style. They are all domestic, but they range from a seventeenth-century Indian palace to a Parisian bathroom of the 1920s. Aesthetically, what unites them is a purity, a completeness, a pervasiveness of their design which has refined each to utter perfection. Each looks back to a different historical period, to a different 'classic' past which informs every gesture, every touch.

Each of these different classic pasts represents some unattainable ideal for the contemporary world to aspire to. Most civilizations have an instinctive tendency to worship their ancestors, an innate reverence for the old, the rare and the precious. You have only to observe our modern hunger for antiques, for period costume dramas, for new historical theories, for visiting ancient ruins or for viewing stately homes, to see this at work today. And beneath all this runs a strong undercurrent of utopianism, as we search for an ideal past as an expression of our hopes for the future.

The details of Giovanna Tornabuoni's dress, hairstyle and accessories in her 1488 portrait by Ghirlandaio, above, and Francesco Venturi's magical photograph of Indian tourists moving through the vast space of Shah Jahan's 1639 Diwan-I-Am in Delhi, left, share a wealth of timeless inspiration and atmosphere. Utterly foreign to each other culturally, historically and geographically, they share a spare, elegant aesthetic that holds great appeal for Allegra and me today.

the renaissance

Although separated by only 30 years, the sophistication of Carpaccio's 1507 Venetian interior, above, has none of the slight naivety of Francesco di Giorgio's design for the Studiolo, opposite. It also remains in its original, magical Venice location, unlike the Studiolo in its air-conditioned sterility at the Metropolitan Museum.

The Renaissance saw the great rebirth of classical knowledge, when famous scholars and artists trawled Italy and the rest of Europe for surviving fragments of the great classical civilizations of Greece and Rome. Very few Renaissance domestic interiors have survived. Our favourite is the Studiolo from the great fortified castle of Gubbio

in Umbria. This was created in around 1480 for Federico da Montefeltro, Duke of Urbino, and is now preserved in the Metropolitan Museum in New York.

The Studiolo was a little gem of an interior, set high up in the castle, a room for the Duke to retire to, not only for reading and study, but also to show off its astounding

craftsmanship, and his own scholarship and learning, to visitors. Its panelling is executed in exquisite intarsia or inlays of different woods in a sophisticated design of false perspective. The upper part of the room, now dispersed, consisted of a painted series of female allegorical figures representing the virtues of the age. The panelling itself is cunningly designed in *trompe l'oeil*, and features references to all the arts and noble attributes that were the contemporary earthly evidence of the virtues painted above.

Two items in particular stand out: Montefeltro's Garter, for he was a Knight of the English order, and had this motif depicted hanging from a shelf and also carved into the stone doorframe of the original room; and a *mazzocchio*, a curious piece of male headgear of the period, doughnut-shaped and faceted, the drawing of which was the mark of a true virtuoso of the new art of perspective. The drawing of perspective, which was the key to the art and architecture of the period, here became part of the decoration of the room.

Perspective also dominates the second image we have chosen. Carpaccio's *Vision of St Augustine*, in the Scuola di San Giorgio degli Schiavoni in Venice shows the scholarly recluse in a perfectly rendered, idealized version of a learned man's study, surrounded by his books and signs of learning. The simplicity of the furniture, the purity of the natural pigment colours and the atmosphere of learning and humanism are all symptomatic of the aspirations of the age. By chance, the colours of the painting — a muted, dull green with terracotta reds — are very similar to the Indian-inspired colours we used in our little house in the country.

There is something so perfectly elegant, spare and refined about the whole composition and the interior. Here is a true minimalism, an interior reduced to a few salient elements. I love the simple, direct details of the furniture, the nailed-on leather and velvet, the ingenious, removable desk and bench that are supported by wall-brackets and single legs — all like small, very human incidents within the grand, symmetrical space. The inspiration of these two spaces, the one real, the other imaginary, is tremendous. Both possess a purity, a singularity that is wonderfully refreshing.

The Duke of Urbino's Studiolo, as reassembled in New York. Almost impossible to photograph, this space still has a great immediacy more than 500 years after its creation.

red fort, delhi

India is crowded with beautiful, extraordinary interiors, but for us the summit of perfection is reached in the apartments of the Red Fort at Delhi, built by Shah Jahan in 1650 as one of the capitals of his vast empire.

The rooms that one visits today were originally only seen by the most intimate members of the royal family and their servants. The extraordinary luxuries of the interior were hidden even from nobles and high officials who were allowed no further than the Diwan I-Am, a crowded hall where the king sat on a high, jewel-encrusted throne to hear petitions and dispense justice.

These rooms are now devoid of all their original furnishings. These consisted not of furniture, but of luxurious tents and drapes of silks, velvets and other precious fabrics. Descendants of the Mongol tents of their ancestors, these drapes, curtains, screens and carpets shut out the harsh Indian sun, the cold desert winds and the prying eyes of nobles and peasants alike. On the carpets, woven from pashmina and silk,

sat mattresses, bolsters, tasselled cushions and cups of rock crystal inlaid with precious stones. What now remain are but the bones of these interiors.

But what bones! One of the rooms in Delhi has an inscription carved into the translucent alabaster wall, a verse composed by Shah Jahan: 'If there be heaven on earth, it is this! It is this! Oh, it is this!' The apartments in each palace were very similar, invariably arranged around a series of gardens, called 'Char-Bagh' or quartered-garden, divided in four by the 'River of Life', or running water channels, to resemble the garden of paradise as described in the Qu'ran. The water channels flowed through the apartments and the length of the palace, which was formed of a string of pavilions set on the edge of a high terrace overlooking the river.

Within the apartments, the water cascaded down curious interior fountains, framed in the centre of a wall like a European fireplace, each consisting of a slanting marble panel with a carved pattern of fishscales that created musical rippling sounds. The water then ran down into a slot in the floor, running beneath it to emerge again in the centre of the room where it played in soft jets in a shallow pool. In the window openings, behind pierced screens, were hung mats of woven vetiver plants, constantly wetted with dripping water to provide cooled,

scented air as the breeze passed through them.

Now all is silent and dry and hot. The more precious of the inlaid stones have been removed from the carved marble flower reliefs, and the rooms are fast disappearing under the destructive strain of the huge number of visitors. But to us they will always remain the most perfect, luxurious, refined spaces in the world, and in a quiet corner, when the wind is just so, you can half-close your eyes and imagine what it must have been.

Allegra and I first saw these rooms on our honeymoon and were totally seduced by the glamour and magic of them, a vision we will never lose.

Two views of the Diwan-I-Am in the Red Fort. The red sandstone walls and columns were originally plastered in the Indian style of A'raish, using Chuna lime polished with stones to give a marble-like sheen. The wall behind the throne-dais has a collection of pietra-dura inlaid marble panels, including one plaque depicting Orpheus playing his lyre, above, probably made at the Grand Ducal workshops in Florence and sent to the Mughals by one of the Medici. The setting is of Indian craftsmanship and typical of the luxurious, floral style of Shah Jahan, who would emerge through the low doorway from the private apartments, surrounded by the court nobles flicking the air with bejewelled fly-whisks.

claude-nicolas ledoux

Claude-Nicolas Ledoux was a hugely talented architect whose working life was cut short by the French Revolution, his best clients being among its most hated figures. After the Revolution, he spent years composing great volumes of 'improved' renderings of his work and visionary projects that could never have been built. As a child, I spent my afternoon rests not in bed but in my father's library, poring over his copies of Ledoux's books, wandering in my mind through his ideal city of Chaux.

Ledoux's most famous works remained unbuilt, existing only as engravings. Designed in a bizarre minimalist classical style, with Assyrian monumentality, these projects – palaces and cottages alike – possess a modernity that is shocking even now. His executed work, mostly now destroyed, was less radical but just as theatrical. The Musée Carnavalet in Paris has a surviving room from his Hôtel d'Uzès of 1767 which displays virtually nothing of the sculptural, abstract quality of the projects. The panelling has extraordinary tree motifs in gilded wood bas-relief,

almost the height of the wall, the trees carved with trophies of the various arts tied to their trunks.

The motif of a tree with an emblem attached goes back to Greek and Roman classical times. Ledoux doubtless took the idea from the classical texts that were so popular in Paris. Simulating a garden in paint on the walls was a popular theme in Roman decoration, but here Ledoux takes

the theme further by contrasting the simple naturalism of the trees with the artificial and contrived gilding and the exquisitely refined and delicate architecture of the room. I like to imagine the space peopled with chattering Parisians wrapped in fashionable Kashmir shawls and cotton dresses printed with Indian 'Tree of Life' motifs.

An important theme in the decorative arts in every civilization,

The boiseries, or panelling, of Ledoux's Hôtel d'Uzes, now installed in that Parisian treasure-trove, the Musée Carnavalet. The carved, gilded trees with hanging trophies were a direct allusion to the classical Greek practice of hanging trophies on a tree beside a shrine.

gardens took on a particular significance in the neo-classical France of the 1780s. An obsession with naturalism, inspired by the writings of Rousseau, a vogue for all things English (including Capability Brown-style gardening) and a reaction to burgeoning mechanization led to garden motifs

appearing everywhere. One curious idea was the garden-room within a garden: a dining room inside a purpose-built 'cottage', painted inside to resemble a path through a wood, giving diners the illusion of being somewhere else.

What is directly inspiring about the Hôtel d'Uzès' room is the way

Ledoux has taken an ancient model and blended it with a contemporary fashion item (the 'Tree of Life' fabric) to produce a wholly new motif. It is this that makes the room neither a pompous, gilded reception room, nor a naturalistic *trompe l'oeil*, but something entirely new.

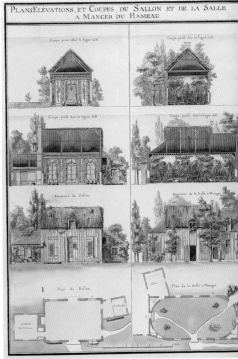

One of Ledoux's sadly vanished interiors, left, his dining room for Mlle Guimard in the Rue de la Chaussée d'Antin, where painted smoke and leaves masked the edges of the mirror-glass set flush with the painted wall over the fireplace. The typically picturesque scheme is of an external terrace with painted walls of trellis, designed to include the real doors and windows of the room, and a low stone balustrade to accommodate the fireplace. Above, designs for a pair of picturesque 'peasant cottages' for the Duc de Condé at Chantilly, in imitation of Marie-Antoinette's Hameau at Versailles, in fact a rather grand ballroom and a dining room.

sir john soane

Soane's great masterpiece, the Bank of England, as completed by him and rendered ruinous by his unfortunate but hugely gifted watercolourist JM Gandy, below, in one of the presentation drawings made for the annual exhibition at the Royal Academy, where Soane lectured in architecture.

Sir John Soane made two breakfast rooms for himself in the adjoining houses in Lincoln's Inn Fields, London, which he left to the nation and are still open as Sir John Soane's Museum. The first, created in 1790 while a young, hopeful architect with two small sons and a wife he adored, had something of a garden theme, with its lightly painted 'trellis' ceiling with a painted sky above. The second, made 30 years later, after his sons had disappointed him and his wife had died, was modelled instead on the interior of an Etruscan tomb chamber he had seen in Italy as a young student. Soane was a strange, obsessive man, fixated on death, who built a museum at the back of his house, around an Egyptian sarcophagus installed in the 'Crypt'.

Despite its morbid inspiration, the later Breakfast Room has to be one of the most beautiful small rooms in the world. Everything about it contributes to an evocation of that eighteenth-century ideal of 'the Sublime'. Soane contrived to model the space in such a way that simply standing in the room gives one a unique and powerful sensation. The flat, handkerchief dome; the cunning side-lighting beyond; the partly yellow glass that creates an aged, moody light; the hundreds of small, convex mirrors and the narrow slips of mirror in cabinets and window frames: all work together to lend the room an intense emotional charge, not exactly sorrowful but certainly sombre.

Soane was completely transformed by his early travels in Italy. He set out as a bright young student, paying for the journey with prize money from a Royal Academy Gold Medal, having worked for several years for various London architects (he was himself the son of a poor Reading bricklayer). Once there, enraptured at embracing for the first time the Roman origins of so much great architecture, he grew obsessed with the domes, the vaults, the details that he saw, measured and drew, with their ruined state and the decay and poignancy that was Rome at that time.

All of this pervades Soane's later work, which focuses on themes of decayed grandeur and

antique fragments. He had drawings made of his projects, such as the Bank of England, his great masterpiece (tragically destroyed by that mediocre architect, Sir Herbert Baker, in 1924), in a ruined state. The Bank was so like an ancient palace, with its warren-like passages and great vaulted halls, that the 'ruin' drawing seems more a work of archaeology than architecture. For security, the building had few external windows, and the resulting top-lighting throughout gave it even more of an ancient feel. Soane also insisted on building his domes and vaults from special conical bricks copied from those he had seen in Rome.

The sepulchral quality of the bank's interiors is best appreciated today in that most magical survivor, his Breakfast Room in Lincoln's Inn Fields, top and in a detail, opposite. The circles in the handkerchief dome's pendentives were originally open holes, which Soane later filled with convex mirrors, giving us this perfect overview. Surrounding the mirror is typical Soane ornament of running beads.

pelagio palagi

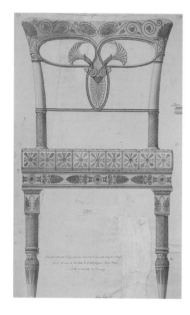

The watercolour design, above, for a chair for the Queen's bedroom at Racconigi shows Palagi's usual obsessive and perfectionist eye for detail, as does that for a small stool, opposite, for the Gabinetto Etrusco, right. This room has Palagi's 'modern' 1830s adaptation of 'Etruscan' (in reality South Italian colonial Greek) motifs from vases in his own collection, applied in every kind of technique from painting and wood inlay to painted glass and a mosaic floor.

A native of Bologna, Pelagio Palagi's greatest success came in 1830s Turin where he was commissioned by Carlo Alberto, King of Sardinia, to design every aspect of the court's aesthetic life, from candelabras and uniforms to stage sets. Like John Soane, Palagi was an enthusiastic antiquarian and collector, and his large collection of Etruscan and Egyptian objects can still be seen in the wonderful museum in Bologna that was built to house it. Palagi took inspiration particularly from the Etruscan finds, creating a series of interiors in the palaces in and around Turin in an energetic, classicizing style all his own.

Turin at that time still housed the workshops that had produced the extraordinary, intricate furniture of the eighteenth century. These workshops, equipped with new machines and techniques, and with the amazingly comprehensive aesthetic of Palagi, produced furniture and rooms that continue to astonish today. There are individual pieces in many major museums (the Victoria & Albert has two chairs, the Met in New York a sofa) but to see the real thing you must go to Turin. The beautiful palace of Racconigi, partly from 1670 and partly from 1760, contains entire suites of rooms entirely by Palagi, who worked there from 1833 to 1842.

The most famous interior of all, the Etruscan Room, was so extraordinary that parts of it – its

doors, desk and floor – were shown at the Crystal Palace Great Exhibition of 1851. The room is made with an intarsia wood inlay technique similar to the Gubbio Studiolo three centuries earlier. The inspiration, too, was similar: the classical world that had just begun to be discovered in 1530 was by now the subject of exhaustive archaeological investigation. Palagi took motifs from his collection of Greek and Etruscan vases and applied them in an elegant though somewhat dry manner to the space. The furniture shares the same motifs and decoration, with the chairs supposedly modelled on classical examples. The forms are, in fact, not like anything classical but their animal feet and deep curves are clearly inspired by the classic.

The museum in Bologna has that unreconstructed quality that is increasingly rare among museums and has been allowed to remain as originally laid out in the mid-nineteenth century. This small, enchanting building was designed around Palagi's collection, by one of his pupils. The display cases and wall decoration are part of an all-embracing concept which lends the interior an excitement similar to the old Egyptian rooms, the Musée Charles X, at the Louvre, before they were sadly altered. Museums around the world are being savagely purged of their original atmosphere in an effort to make them more politically correct and

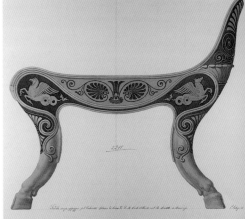

better 'edutainment'. This is one of the great tragedies of our time. The joys of discovery and of unexpected juxtapositions are vanishing forever. The hugely inspiring, chaotic displays of old, with objects packed tightly against each other, with drawers of similar items ready for the interested few to open, are giving way to didactic presentations that allow no room for imagination or inspiration.

In the late nineteenth century, the archaeological inspiration of Palagi's work, which had developed from the neo-classical styles of Ledoux and his contemporaries, blossomed into attempts at creating entire environments of 'authentic' classical decoration. Most of these have now disappeared but one fabulous example, begun as a private villa but destined before completion to become a kind of museum that is still open today, remains at Beaulieu-sur-Mer on the French Riviera (see page 26).

villa kerylos, beaulieu

The Villa Kerylos was the creation of Theodore Reinach, an eccentric antiquarian scholar, and his wife. Together, from 1903, they constructed this extraordinary villa in which everything, from the architecture and decoration down to the cutlery, was modelled on classical Greek examples. What is fascinating today is the strange marriage of ancient Greek style and *fin-de-siècle* Parisian technology, featuring bizarre combinations such as an upright piano covered with marquetry of Greek design, and the mosaic-walled shower with an antiqued bronze shower head.

The furniture, made by two of the most sophisticated Paris workshops of the time, is of exceptional quality; it is most intriguing for being modelled closely on ancient examples but with an insistence on modern comfort. All the upholstery and the wall-hangings of embroidered linen with Greek motifs were made by hand, using stitches thought to be authentically ancient; the details throughout are exquisitely made, including tiny, cast bronze hooks to hang the embroideries from.

This archaeological style was hugely popular at the time, as a quick glance at late Victorian paintings will show. In London Sir Lawrence Alma-Tadema commissioned 'ancient' furniture like his beautiful Greek/Egyptian couch (now in London's V&A Museum), Greek on one side, Egyptian on the other, suitable for use in paintings of either era. The Villa Kerylos, however, remains unique in its comprehensiveness, its thoroughness, as well as in having survived intact.

My father adored the Villa Kerylos and took me there every summer as a child; mesmerized by anything to do with the Greece of Alexander the Great, I adored it too. I took Allegra there when we were first married and something about the totality of its decoration, the intense feeling of the interior, the subtle beauty of the embroideries against the painted walls inspired us both. We have never used any motifs from the house, or tried to copy its rooms, but we have attempted to capture its spirit and atmosphere in our own work.

Two views of the Villa Kerylos: left, a detail of the painted decoration adapted, like the rest of the house, from Greek motifs, here anthemion scrolls; above, Mme Reinach's bedroom, with coarsely embroidered curtains and hangings in rough linen seeking an ancient authenticity. In a similar way, the bed is simply made with leather straps on a wood frame, with a wool mattress. Ironically enough, this simplicity was created by the most sophisticated workshops of fin-de-siècle Paris.

villa of the mysteries, pompeii

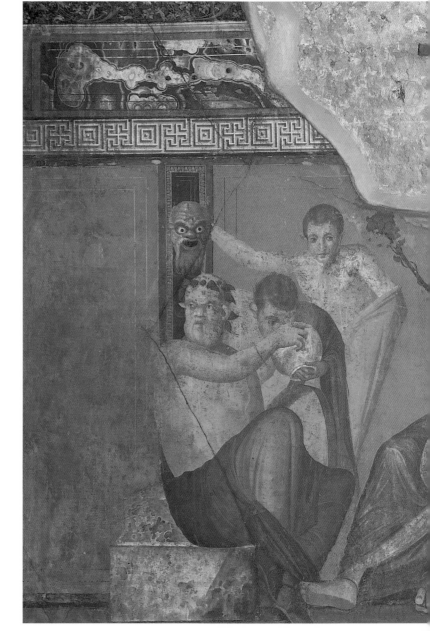

While all of these interiors look back to a distant and idealized past, we might expect that the miraculously preserved villas of Pompeii, shrouded for nearly two thousand years in volcanic ash, would not. But of course the artists, designers and clients of the Roman Empire were every bit as inspired by the past as were their imitators in later years.

The Romans imitated the Greeks: much of Roman art, indeed, is famously derivative of superb and sadly lost Greek originals. The great eras of Praxiteles and Phidias were viewed by Romans as an almost mythical Golden Age, yearned for with an obsessiveness comparable to the Pre-Raphaelites' feeling for the early Renaissance. Greek panel-paintings, as well as their sculptures, were brought to Rome where they took pride of place in the imperial and lesser collections, and whole decorative and pictorial schemes were derived from written descriptions of lost masterpieces.

The Romans developed their own styles, of course, just as the Greeks had developed theirs, starting from their own archaic

beginnings. The tradition of mural painting, with its complex architectural *trompe l'oeils* and systems for dividing walls, was one of the Romans' most original artistic creations. Examples have survived only where they were buried, and little remains outside this small city beneath Vesuvius.

The discovery of Pompeii in the eighteenth century prompted a new vogue for imitations of its painted rooms, to be revived and given fresh impetus by the novelty of colour printing in the 1840s when lithographs of Pompeian murals were copied on to walls throughout Europe. Occasionally, when handled by original and talented designers such as Karl Friedrich Schinkel in Berlin, the results were a success. On the whole, however, they were rather poor, like many of the originals.

The great masterpiece of Pompeii is not exactly a domestic interior, but its intimate scale means that the famous interior of the Villa of the Mysteries fits our scheme. Its painted frieze of a Dionysian initiation rite, featuring a woman celebrating a 'marriage'

with the god, was copied from a Greek original, and the powerful figures have the grace of Greek sculpture. It is an extraordinary feeling to stand in this room, with its figures cavorting against the vibrant red ground, and to sense

the life that still pulsates from the walls two thousand years later.

What inspires us here, once again, is the atmosphere, the intensity of design, and the all-embracing quality. The details, so perfectly integrated and resolved;

the illusion, so complete and bewitching; the sense of place, human scale, symmetry, colour: all are sublime and perfect. What these spaces must have been like filled with drunken, over-painted Roman matrons decked with gold jewellery, lying around on gaudily decorated couches and screeching at slaves to bring more wine, is perhaps best not imagined: the ruins as they have survived are so wonderfully beautiful, so clean, so sober, an inspiration for all time.

The extraordinary frescoes of the Villa of the Mysteries caused a sensation when they were revealed in 1909. The exact function of both room and imagery are much debated, but their sheer beauty remains indisputable.

armand albert rateau

Paris between the two world wars was home to a tremendous concentration of artistic talent in every sphere. Design and decoration here reached a peak of sophistication and variety unique in history, embracing everything from the machine aesthetic of Le Corbusier to the decadent styles of Sue et Mare. A series of exhibitions by the Union des Artistes Décorateurs showed off this talent to the world, with a unique blend of cultural influences that embraced both archaeological finds on view in the great museums and ethnic art from French colonies in Africa and the Pacific.

These twin inspirations combined to fuel the work of one of the most astounding designers of the time, Armand Albert Rateau. He worked little and for few clients, but his creations were on a scale and with a level of detail that is still astonishing. His major commissions were for the Duchess of Alba in Madrid; for the Blumenthals in New York, where he created a fantasy swimming pool with chairs made of linked bronze fish; at Leeds Castle in Kent; and most importantly, for *couturière* Jeanne Lanvin.

The bedroom suite from Lanvin's house on Rue Barbet de Jouy, created in 1920, survives in the Musée des Arts Décoratifs, on the Rue de Rivoli, in Paris. The bedroom itself is an exquisite space, hung with a mauve silk with white decoration in a slightly Art Nouveau style; but it is the bathroom, made entirely from stone and bronze, that is the most striking and that we have found most inspiring.

One of the great strengths of the Paris decorating scene of the time was the proliferation of small workshops of incredible skill. Virtually every kind of craft was either still practised from the days of the Ancien Régime, or was being invented afresh, as in the famous lacquer workshops where Jean Dunand revived the ancient Chinese art. Rateau had his own workshops, as did most important decorators, which produced all of the furniture, panelling, lamps, fabrics and trimmings that he required. In 1929, they employed no fewer than 212 artisans.

The rooms abound with lively and exquisite detail, most notably the bronze mounts of mirrors, taps, handles, lamps, soap dishes and so on. Cast in bronze after Rateau's sketches, these display a concentration on detail owing

something to the designer's early career in jewellery design. His style is hard to place, blending historical sources as eclectic as ancient Assyrian, African tribal and Byzantine with a modern crispness and elegance. Simplicity and understatement are here allied with the most outrageous luxury.

For us it is the completeness of the work, the potency of the atmosphere, the quality of the craftsmanship, the assimilation of so many styles and periods, and the ahistorical approach that make Rateau so inspiring. The intricate signature details in cast bronze and the unique embroideries and mouldings we have attempted ourselves, in shy imitation of a great master.

The bathroom of the great fashion designer Jeanne Lanvin, thankfully rescued before the demolition of her apartment in Paris and now preserved for us all to enjoy at the Musée des Arts Décoratifs. It has a timeless chic and beauty, and will doubtless look every bit as modern in the next century as it does now, and every bit as other-worldly too, with its intricately hand-crafted bronze details and the seemingly effortless curves of the carved stone wash basin and bathtub.

brook house, london

Sir Ernest Cassell's jade collection, above, in one of a pair of slightly Chinese, slightly Deco, very modern vitrines in the drawing-room. Opposite, the long hall that led from the private elevator to the street. The curtains from the great, high window on the stairs, woven in linen and embroidered in silver thread, are now in our own home.

My grandmother Edwina Mountbatten inherited a huge Victorian mansion, Brook House on Park Lane, from her grandfather, the financier Sir Ernest Cassell. In 1937 she sold it to a property developer who demolished the house, putting up a new, plain brick building of offices and apartments on the site . My grandparents rented the top two floors of this building as their London home, with an express elevator straight from the street. It was the most modern house in London at the time, and one of the most stylish.

A New York designer, Mrs Joshua Cosden, was hired to decorate the apartment, and took on the difficult task of producing a streamlined, modern interior to house the Cassell collection which had formerly been displayed in rooms with wall paintings by Boucher and Fragonard and heavy with Victorian marble and velvets. My grandmother had hated the old house, describing it as a 'marble mausoleum', and after living in it for eighteen years was determined to have something quite different

and modern, like the stylish apartments of her circle in New York or English friends such as Philip Sassoon at Port Lympne.

The new Brook House was a triumph. Long terraces wrapped around the apartment, offering open views of Hyde Park, while an enfilade of reception rooms could be separated by sliding doors or opened up to provide a setting for large receptions and dances, or the impromptu cinema shows that my grandfather liked to give after someone else's dinner party. The whole thing was hugely glamorous but short-lived, for they closed the house up at the outbreak of war in 1939, never to return.

For all the brevity of its heyday, the apartment was an unusually complete and sophisticated London interior for its time, when most grand houses were extremely old-fashioned and the new ones, with rare exceptions, very traditional. The manner in which the collection (now sadly dispersed) was displayed in the new sparsely decorated rooms was exceptionally successful, as the surviving photographs show.

The masses of Chinese jade and old English silver were shown off in new, chic vitrines with subtle Art Deco lines and the latest lighting, while around them the emphasis was on materials, with silver-leafed ceilings and calf-skin doors.

Just before Allegra and I married, we went to Brook House (then about to be demolished) with my parents. Converted into offices of unspeakable dreariness, it was hard to make out the beautiful swan of these pictures in the partitioned-up ugly duckling that remained. Then, when we were decorating our own house in London, we found some wonderful old curtains languishing in a barn in the country, which turned out to have come from the high windows on the stairs at Brook House. They had been woven by Marion Dorn, a famous rug and textile designer of the 1930s, who worked extensively for Syrie Maugham and other decorators, and also made several rugs for the apartment. These curtains now hang in our own tiny dining room, and inspired its colouring.

david hicks and jean-michel frank

My own father's work was naturally what surrounded me as a child, both through the houses that he created for us and through his own talk and letters, which kept me more involved with his career from an early age than many children might have been. He was obsessed with expanding his design 'empire', opening David Hicks shops across Europe, publishing book after book of his work, putting his 'H' logo on everything (including the bed sheets in which I slept) and making bizarre drawings to illustrate the growing range of his business, with trees or puppet-strings to show the offshoots.

Recently, while cataloguing the photographic archive of his work, I discovered a curious anomaly: among thousands of large-format transparencies of his best work from the 1960s and 70s were three pictures of another man's work. Taken in the early 70s by a photographer who was in Paris to shoot a Hicks project for *David Hicks on Decoration-5*, the photographs (which were not for publication, but for my father's own interest) showed the Paris living room of the Vicomte de Noailles, decorated in the 1930s by Jean-Michel Frank.

Jean-Michel Frank is probably the single most influential designer

of the last decade. He worked for barely ten years, with his brilliant but unrecognized partner Adolphe Chanaux, starting with his own apartment which he had hired Chanaux to execute in 1930. His career ended with the closure of his fashionable Faubourg St Honoré shop and his own flight from Paris and the advancing Germans, who would doubtless have murdered this brilliant Jewish artist in a death camp. Instead he took his own life in New York in 1941.

Frank was a kind of minimalist, taking grand nineteenth-century apartments, stripping them to their bare bones, installing expanses of luxurious but simple natural materials such as straw marquetry, ray-skin and parchment, and furnishing the rooms with his own designs. Some of these pieces were abstracted from eighteenth-century originals reduced to their essentials, while others were in a sharp, geometric, cubist style, a reduced Art Deco. Contrasting with this are flowery touches, carpets and screens by Christian Bérard and plaster lights by the Giacometti brothers. The work is rich in allusions to the past, but also fresh and new; today it looks completely undated, with a relaxed, comfortable air that is totally liveable.

My father admired Frank hugely, although his own work was utterly different (he also admired William Kent and Philip Johnson). He did occasionally do Frankish things, such as cladding a dining room in stainless steel panels, or a living room with walls of sewn suede. But where Frank was a master of subtlety, my father was above all dramatic. Every room had to make a big impression, to be slightly overwhelming, as though it was under a spell that must never be broken. Relaxing? No. Occasionally intimidating,

always perfect and incredibly stylish. It was a grand, formal, graphic style, rather like the seventeenth- and eighteenth-century, but with modern elements.

The 'Long Room' at Britwell, opposite, where I grew up, decorated by my father in 1973 in a scheme of violently clashing pinks and reds. The textured carpet is his design; the walls are pink felt. The Noailles' living room in Paris, above, with the Frank furniture covered in white cotton summer slipcovers.

classical influences in the modern interior

It is never very easy to identify your own influences. Small things are not hard to spot: a fragment of a pattern that was adapted for a fabric, a memory of ripples on water that became a rug design, a synthesis of different half-remembered old tables and a gap in someone's living room that prompted a new furniture piece. But the sources for the larger picture, the more subtle, mysterious process of putting together a whole scheme of decor and furnishing – these are the ones that are more difficult to pinpoint.

This chapter has presented a succession of beautiful interiors that have been a tremendous inspiration to us. When Allegra and I met, we had wide-ranging, almost all-encompassing tastes, for we had grown up in very strongly designed but dramatically different houses, had learned a certain attitude from our parents that was then quite changed by art and design schools, and had started to work on our own, which of course is the strongest formative influence of all.

Together we rediscovered the past, found the inspiration of the classic. Allegra opened my eyes to the 50s, that dread decade that my father had loathed; I introduced her to the joys of neo-classicism, and so on. We went together to India, a whole subcontinent of inspiration that we had both dreamed of seeing. It has been an adventure, a voyage of discovery. What we have shown in this chapter are brief glimpses, moments from that voyage, stops on the way. There are occasional direct inspirations but more often they are indirect and imprecise. What we have drawn from these rooms is an atmosphere of completeness, luxury, timelessness and a rootedness in history, an inspiration from the past. This is what we have attempted to reflect in our own modest creations, using the materials available to us now.

Our living room in London. On the left, my 'Drum' table; in the centre, one with copper leaves holding a parchment top, designed by Allegra. Surrounding the portrait of Edward VII are drawings by Anish Kapoor and a fragment of a Coptic Egyptian tunic.

design evolution

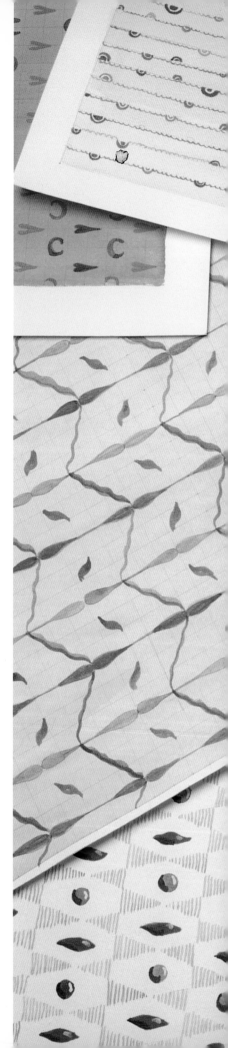

H aving made the selection of historical interiors that formed the last chapter, Allegra and I wanted to find a way of presenting the other influences that we draw on when creating interiors and designing

products. These influences are extremely broad, almost arbitrary, in that they are divided neither by date, nor by style, nor by region. We immediately thought of the Pitt Rivers Museum in Oxford, where the largely ethnographic displays include objects from ancient Egypt, nineteenth-century Europe and Japan, making it far broader in scope than any conventional museum of ethnography.

My sketch for the 'Drum' table, and some of Allegra's watercolour designs for rug and fabric patterns. The design at bottom left was the first to be woven as a rug, commissioned by a client for her studio apartment in London.

are grouped together, adjacent to board games, whether from ancient Egypt or eighteenth-century Italy or Britain. The same is true for baskets, guns, armour, fishing tackle, clothing – the list is endless – of every kind and every culture.

The excitement of the museum lies precisely in this juxtaposition of objects separated in time and space but related through pattern, colour, texture – all the fingerprints that peoples everywhere leave on their artefacts. The surprise of these similarities, the wealth of pattern and ornament, the exotic and fabulous materials: armour made from giant sea urchins, feather cloaks, eskimo coats of transparent sealskin, necklaces of tiny exotic birds; all this represents a whole world of inspiration, combined, for us, with the heritage of Western decorative arts, including the interiors in the previous chapter, and the wealth of furniture, textiles and objects that survives from every period. That said, Allegra and I work in quite different ways. While I am fascinated by specific cultural and historical forms, and draw on them quite directly, she works in a more intuitive way, assimilating images and influences and creating patterns and forms of her own without specific sources.

This chapter looks at eleven of our products, at their inspirations and development, and their links to the rest of our work. We both love to go through old pattern books, poring over drawers of old

fragments at museums like the Victoria & Albert in London and the Musée des Tissus in Lyons. We voraciously collect books on old textiles and costume, and look at whatever we can when we travel.

Indian textiles are a huge source of inspiration. The small collection at the National Museum in New Delhi contains unbelievable pieces, mainly male costumes, with belts embroidered with gold thread and beetlewings, shawls printed with silver and woven silk velvet. The intricacy of the work and the subtlety of the colours are breathtaking. The City Palace Museum in Jaipur displays the old Palace wardrobes together with exquisite carpets of the Moghul era.

Another great fund of imagery is Renaissance painting, which shows clothing and furnishings made from precious and valuable fabrics. The dresses of sixteenth- and seventeenth-century court portraits, where precious stones were sewn on to a dress for one event and removed afterwards, are a reminder of a time when such fabrics were treated as settings for jewels. The damasks and other weaves possess a simplicity and boldness that remain undiluted.

These historical sources are immensely inspiring, but in a general, non-specific way. In a world of computer design, Allegra stubbornly draws her own designs free-hand in watercolour, blending and mixing the inspirations that she has been absorbing to inform the

A typically bizarre group of objects, above, in a vitrine at the Pitt Rivers Museum in Oxford. The intimate, cluttered, inspirational quality of the collection is enhanced by the careful, hand-written cards, often still in the hand of Pitt Rivers' first curator, Arthur Balfour. Opposite, in this portrait by Baldovinetti, circa 1465, the intricate hairstyle and the dress, especially the family emblem on the sleeve, are truly inspirational.

The fascination of the Pitt Rivers lies not only in the eclectic nature of its collections, but its unique manner of display. Unchanged since the early years of the twentieth century, it adheres to the principles of its founder, the eccentric General Pitt Rivers, who applied Darwinist evolutionary theory to cultural artefacts. In the museum, objects are arranged by type, regardless of date or region: playing cards, whether European, Indian or Chinese, and whatever their date,

new design in an unconscious, natural way. These influences may include non-textile sources, from botanical illustrations to biology diagrams, from ethnic patterns to a old tree in a fashion photograph. Thus the finished design, having its origin in no particular culture or era, harmonizes with a huge variety of different styles.

But the most fertile source of discovery comes not from taking in but from putting out, from the act of drawing itself. Only when Allegra is seated with a fresh sheet of paper, letting the pattern reveal itself through aimless sketching in light pencil, only then do all of the various ingredients gel, emerging in the form of a new pattern that combines many aspects of different sources, that alludes to this era or that, but is a new pattern itself.

The process is not much different in my own work. My early life was spent immersed in books, trawling through every culture and era, at first guided by my father's passions and prejudices. Then, in deliberate revolt from this world of 'good taste', I started to look at other things, such as tribal art, Japanese art and modern architecture. I have an overwhelming passion for the layering of history, the overlap of cultures, for all of the soft edges where interesting accidents occur. In its fusing of unlikely partners – Greek, African, 1790s and 1930s French, and so on – my furniture shows something of this.

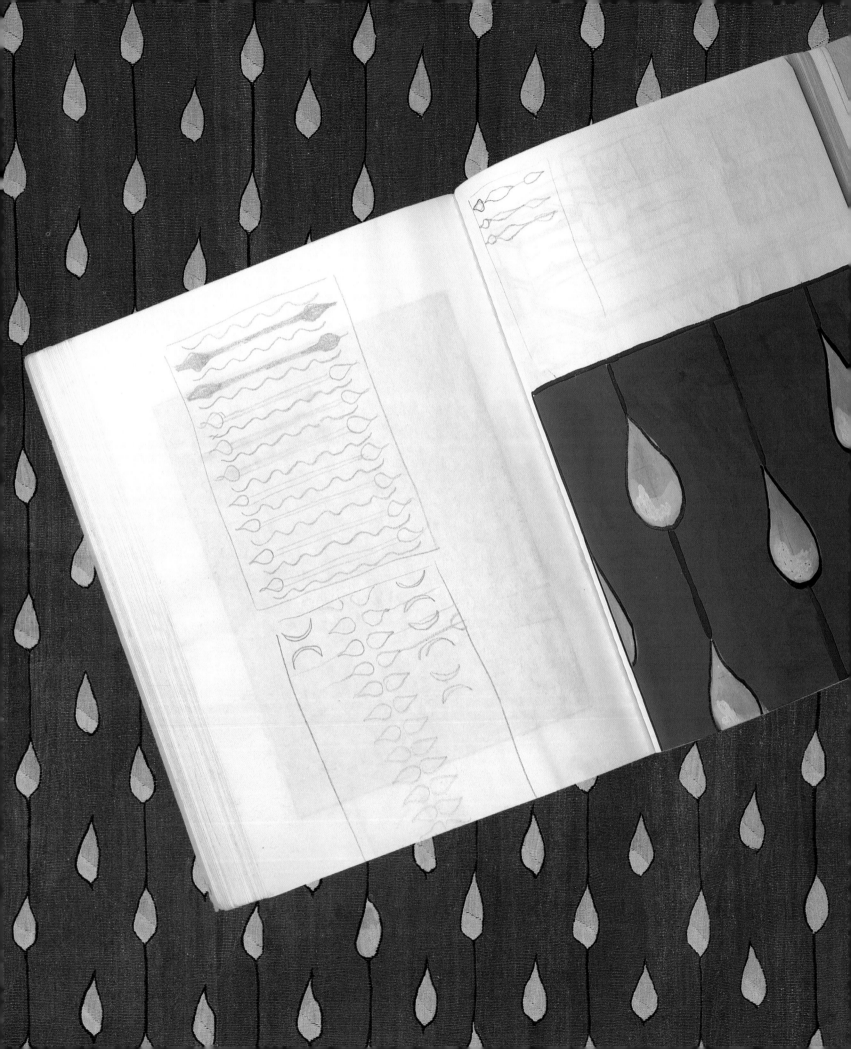

rain

Allegra's 'Rain' kilim, with a first, full-size detail drawing for it in one of her sketchbooks. On the right, an engraving from Barchusen's *Elementa Chemicae*, published in Leiden in 1718, with alchemical emblems illustrating stages in the 'great work'; on the right, drops of alchemical dew captured in the phial. The precise meanings of these emblems hold a great fascination for learned scholars of the arcane, while we are more interested in their abstract, formal qualities which we find hugely provocative and inspiring.

Allegra's very first pattern design was 'Rain', a pattern of drops falling, marshalled into lines, which could well have derived from seventeenth-century motifs of dew falling in an alchemical treatise, or teardrops in enamel on a mourning ring of 1680. In fact, the drops simply arrived in a sketch, a fortuitous discovery. There is something of the garden in this image of welcome rain, something very much in the tradition of the great Moghul carpets depicting gardens, but at the same time it is very modern.

Allegra had been designing patterns without any specific plan for producing them. By chance one of our clients saw another of these first designs and wanted to commission it as a rug for her apartment. We approached Christopher Farr, who with his partner Matthew Bourne produces flat-weave kilims and hand-knotted rugs of astonishing quality in Turkey, and ordered the first rug. Christopher proposed that Allegra should design a collection for him.

This collection included the 'Rain' design and twelve others, some kilims, some rugs. Using his great experience, Christopher was able to edit Allegra's designs, to select what would work and what would not, and to explain why certain patterns could not be woven as kilims (because of the direction of the weaving, which allows curves in only one direction). The drawings were sent off to Turkey, and four or five months later, back came these extraordinary rugs. The original drawings had been woven with traditionally hand-dyed, oily, natural wool, which gave the colours a delicate, striated quality that magically preserved the 'watercolour' look of Allegra's designs.

The inspirations behind Allegra's designs embrace all of her textile work, including her rugs. Rugs are, however, quite different from fabrics in both nature and function, and Allegra's use of each motif and each influence is necessarily modified by this. Fabrics are versatile in their uses, covering furniture and screening windows in numerous different ways, while patterned textiles often serve the useful function of hiding a stain or two. Rugs, on the other hand, will make a hard floor soft and a cold floor warm; beyond this, their usefulness is somewhat limited.

4 3

sounds

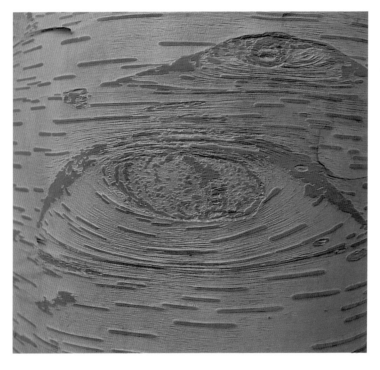

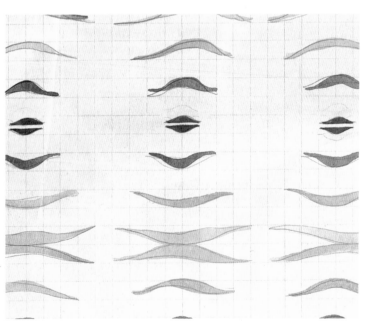

Historically, rugs are the only true survivors from the age of portable possessions, when houses were shells to be 'furnished' only temporarily while they were occupied. Their owners moved from one house to another with their baggage, including much of their furniture and their tapestries and carpets. Only in the late seventeenth century did Louis XIV commission the first pieces of furniture that were not expected to travel constantly, and thus required to be entirely portable. Until the advent of fitted carpets around 1820, rugs were hugely important. Those who could not afford a real carpet would buy a painted floorcloth; but for those whose budget allowed it, a rug was the only thing.

Carpets originated in the East where framed furniture barely existed. In Persia and India, where in the seventeenth century the greatest masterpieces of carpet-making were created in the Moghul factories at Agra and Lahore, furnishings were exclusively soft. It was a matter of laying out striped cotton rugs or dhurries on marble or plaster floors, followed by fine silk, wool and pashmina carpets, and finally cushions and bolsters. Never was there greater comfort. When European traders and colonial officers arrived with their awkward, upright chairs, the Indian courts adopted them slowly, wrapping them in silver or ivory, sitting stiffly for group portraits and

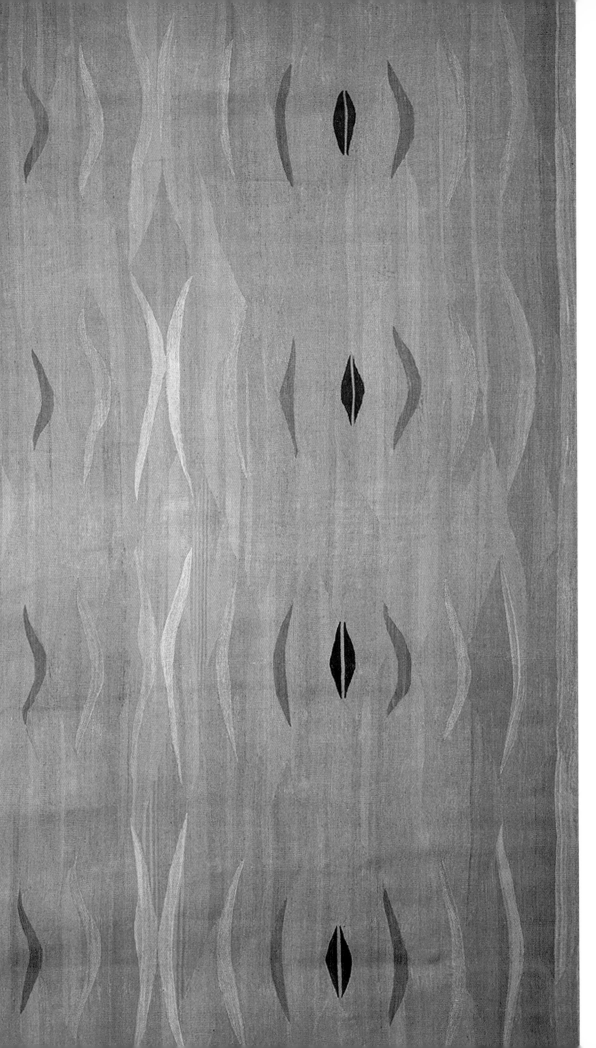

then, doubtless, retiring with relief to their traditional and more luxurious cushions and carpets.

Carpets possess an intrinsic quality of establishing a smaller, more intimate space within a room. They define an area, often an idealized space within the larger, more confused shape of the interior. Those great Indian carpets and their Persian antecedents took this to a logical conclusion by using garden imagery, setting within a border that defined the ideal space, a stylized vision of the Paradise garden that is central to Islamic belief.

Allegra has now designed three collections of rugs with Christopher Farr. Their painterly feel, their traditional form and structure (with all-over patterns and borders) and their sympathetic colour schemes have contributed to their huge success in every kind of interior. For our own decorating clients and those of other designers, Allegra designs special commission rugs and kilims, working around specific furnishing layouts and colour schemes.

The design for 'Sounds', together with a detail of the finished rug, bottom left, showing how well the delicate watercolour look has been captured by the Turkish weavers' hand-dyed wool. Top left, a detail of tree-bark. Allegra's designs are rarely specifically drawn from any one source, but the inspiration of tree markings can be seen here.

slipping

In 1999, keen to produce a more affordable collection of rugs to run alongside Christopher Farr's 'couture' line. we chose to adopt the traditional Indian dhurry technique of cotton flat-weaves. Traditionally used as under-carpets, these had been revived in a big way in the 60s and 70s with new floral and geometric designs in pretty pastel colours. Before this, the main production of dhurries had been confined to gaols across India, where huge rugs were made to floor the vast tents put up for maharajahs whenever they entertained *en masse*.

Allegra was keen to try the dhurry technique partly because of her love of India and the affinity she felt for flat-weave rugs, and partly because the lower costs involved would allow the new collection to be accessible to a wider market. With this in mind, we decided to limit the size of the collection to only ten designs, and to make each in a single standard size and colourway. The designs share the spirit of the other rug collections, although the weave does allow full curves and circles,

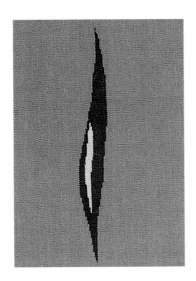

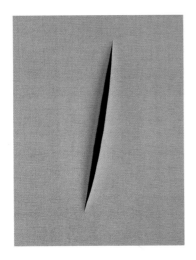

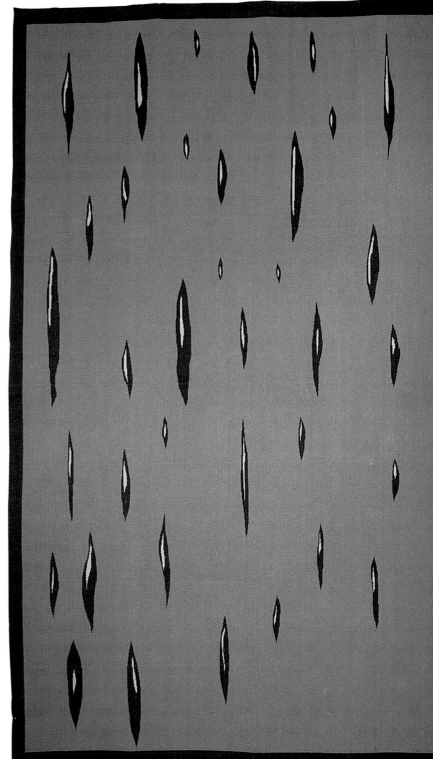

unlike the directional structure of Turkish kilims. The quality is also very different and rather cruder, and the dhurries cannot achieve the wonderful watercolour-like striated look of kilims.

These designs have no precedent at all in the dhurry-weaving tradition. While other types of rug have been the subject of repeated experimentation, dhurries have always traditionally been restricted to plain colours with a border, stripes, geometric designs and highly stylized floral patterns, and more recently Aubusson-style floral designs. Allegra's hand-drawn, painterly but abstract designs were something quite new. Here the cotton weave has something of a rough artist's canvas about it: the rugs are like huge abstract paintings, with straightish lines that wobble and move like brushstrokes.

The colours are taken from the same natural, earthy palette that Allegra had developed in her fabrics and earlier rugs, far-removed from both the pretty pastel pinks and yellows of recent dhurry production and the bright,

Two inspirations for the 'Slipping' rug, right, are the slashing of fabric, seen in Renaissance costume and as shown in the extravagant outfit worn by Baudoin of Burgundy in his 1525 portrait by Mabuse, opposite, and Lucio Fontana's series of 'Spatial Concepts' from 1967, above. There are many possible inspirations for these designs, many competing sources, but these are the more obvious among a larger group.

spheres

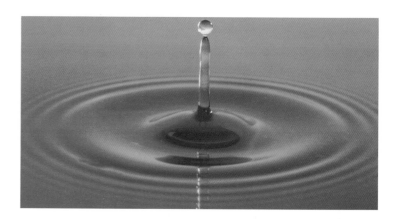

Left, a selection of kaftans of Allegra's design with, below, the hem of one embroidered with an adaptation of the 'Spheres' design. The kaftans began as a sideline, prompted by a friend's embroidery workshop and her enthusiasm for Allegra's designs. This has now grown into a small fashion collection available from our London shop.

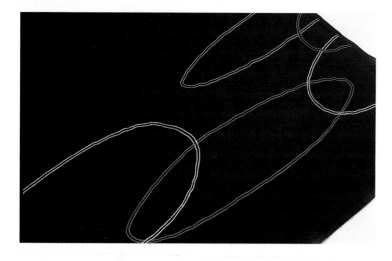

'Spheres', opposite, another dhurry woven in India by craftsmen whose families have been weaving for many generations but who had never before attempted any free-form curved design. The design resembles ripples on water or

floating bubbles, hence the water drop image, right. These designs are made more interesting by being so unspecific about their sources. They allude to a variety of different images and have many possible meanings, but are also simple, decorative patterns.

chemical colours of so many new rugs. These dhurries harmonize wonderfully not only with our furniture and fabrics but also with antique pieces, natural wood floors, stone and natural linen. The rugs are painstakingly hand-made using hand-dyed cotton; and the resulting pieces, with their imagery of abstracted natural forms and their earthy palette, are potent reflections of today's quest for an organic lifestyle.

Allegra's work forms part of a long tradition of deriving patterns from natural forms, going back to the earliest times. Now that many city-dwellers (in climatically benign Europe, at least) are so isolated from nature by new technology in all its forms, many people feel a strong need for a new contact with the natural world beyond the urban sprawl. Hand in hand with this goes a desire for hand-made traditional techniques and artefacts that are not totally standardized

and identical or obviously mass-produced by machine.

While most design work is now done on computer, Allegra is there with her watercolour pad and brush, drawing in a way that people have done since time immemorial, using her hands to produce what her eyes can see. The connection between this hand-drawing and the later hand-making of the finished pieces is integral to the process.

Allegra's feeling for natural, organic forms leads her to search them out, in ethnic art, in historic sources, and in natural forms themselves. A leaf, a twig, a pebble, the markings on a small shell or on a fish glimpsed during a Saturday morning visit to the aquarium; the pitted texture of rough stone; the constantly changing cloudy sky: wherever you look, nature twists and turns itself into new forms, all of which might suggest any number of new patterns.

tree of life

The prototypes of Allegra's fabric designs were first created using traditional hand-block printing in Jaipur. We were visiting friends in the region, and had taken with us Allegra's first collection of patterns, thinking there might just be a chance that we would find someone able to print them. As it happened (and as it so often happens in India), one of our friends had a cousin with a printing workshop; within a few days, we had before us 48 hand-carved wooden printing blocks, exquisitely made exactly to Allegra's watercolour designs. She then spent three days printing first samples of the designs, trying different colourways, watching as the skilled printers laid down colour after colour with the wooden blocks, each measuring roughly four by six inches.

Several of the fabrics were given their names by the printers in Jaipur. As they worked, they gave the patterns names in Hindi, like 'Kali' for one that reminded them of the goddess Kali's fierce-looking eyebrows, and 'Muskan' for a design that resembled a moustache. Partly because the patterns are not Indian in inspiration, Allegra kept the names as a tribute to the skilled Indian printers who had first made them a reality.

Part of the beauty of the hand-block process is the small size of the printing blocks, which results in a beautifully hand-made look and feel. Although for logistical reasons final production of the fabrics had to be done by hand screen-printing in the UK, we were determined to preserve this hand-made feel. We had the new, large screens made from the hand-blocked fabric samples, so that they retained the many little imperfections and irregularities of the originals.

Some patterns have historic meanings that are still relevant and readable today, such as the classic 'Tree of Life' which stretches back at least as far as the ancient Sumerian civilization of 2000BC and appears in almost every culture and every technique thereafter. The various meanings of the design have been reinvented by each culture that used it, but the essential concept of a tree that brings forth life, a plant as symbol of life, is as strong today as it ever was. Allegra reinterpreted this in several rug designs and a fabric.

Allegra's 'Tree of Life' fabric appears on page 76. Here are two rug designs with other versions of this timeless motif, together with an traditional eighteenth-century Indian painted cotton piece, above. Right, an early design for a hand-knotted rug by Allegra for Christopher Farr. Opposite, 'Desert Grass', a kilim from a collection designed by 'Allegra Hicks for Holly Hunt', another take on the theme of 'Tree of Life'.

cintamani embroidery

Once you identify this seemingly obscure pattern, you will find it in the clothes on Moghul miniatures, in jewellery, in tiles, in carpets. As with many essential, archetypal designs, it soon becomes part of your visual vocabulary, leaping out at you like the face of a friend in a crowded room. Today it is simply a wonderful, bold design. We copied a Turkish cut-velvet example in paint on our own dining-room walls, and adapted the design again for a painted mosaic frieze in the house of clients in Switzerland.

Again in India, we found a wonderful embroidery workshop where we made a small collection of cushions and throws with patterns embroidered onto silk or delicate wool. As usual, the designs were inspired by a variety of sources, including one with alchemical emblems. Embroidery has the surprising quality of trembling on the brink of three-dimensionality, the raised stitching of the silk embroidery threads throwing the pattern into very slight relief. The motifs seem to float on the cloth.

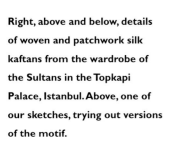

Right, above and below, details of woven and patchwork silk kaftans from the wardrobe of the Sultans in the Topkapi Palace, Istanbul. Above, one of our sketches, trying out versions of the motif.

Some historic patterns have lost the meanings they once held but remain visually strong and exciting, such as the 'Cintamani' of Ottoman velvets (and tiles, carpets and embroidery). This was a royal symbol borrowed by the Turkish sultans from the Moghul emperors of India, who in turn inherited it from their ancestor Timur (Tamerlaine). In the thirteenth century he had used stylized tiger markings as his personal emblem; these evolved into two moustache-like stripes and three balls.

This kind of historic pattern is a delight to work with, as it can be copied faithfully from an original or be so abstracted from it that the connection becomes tenuous. Because the original is far from well-known and anyway has a very modern look, the perfect copy never seems derivative; on the other hand, the more distantly inspired version, as in our cushion, has just enough of the original to share some of its history and associations.

Making these pieces led Allegra to design a collection of kaftans and embroidered shawls. These are beautiful 'non-fashion', relaxed clothes using her trademark patterns and jewel-like colours.

A silk cushion and a wool shawl, right, embroidered with our adaptations of the ancient 'Cintamani' pattern. This is much looser and more freehand than the traditional, rigid repeat which adorned the costumes, interiors and artefacts of Islamic rulers for centuries, and has none of the significance of its tiger-stripe origins.

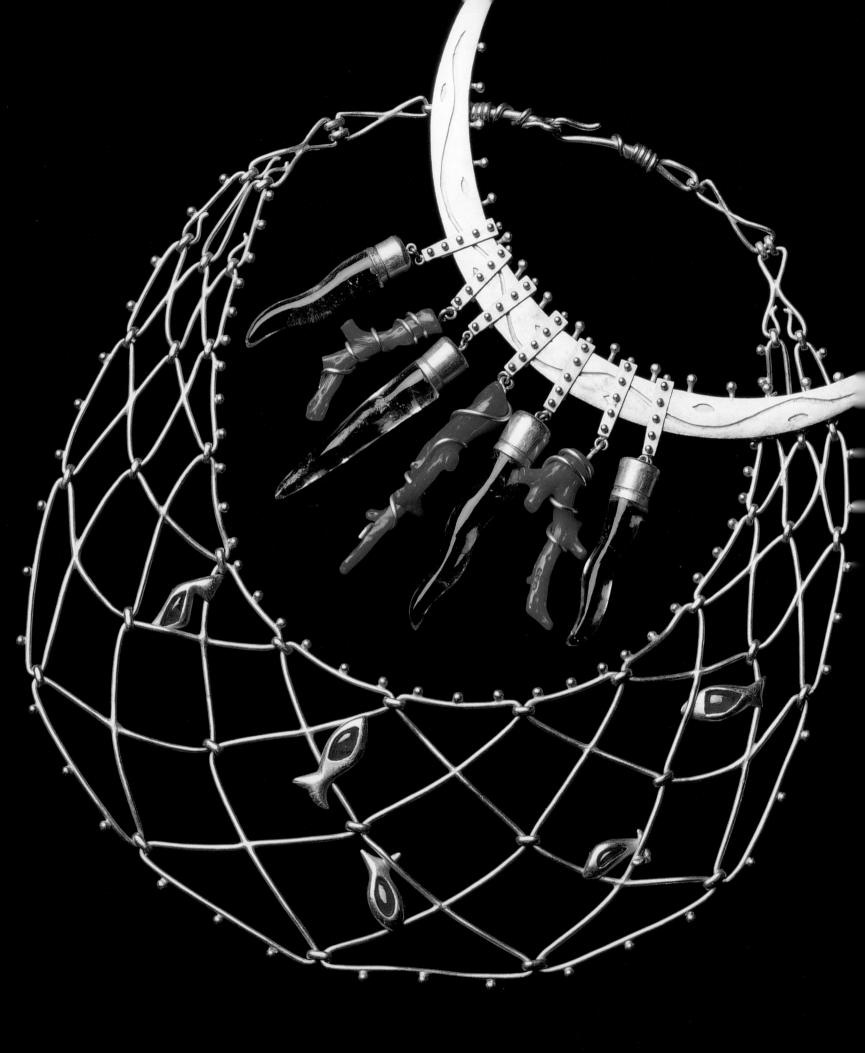

jewellery

I have always loved jewellery and have designed a couple of rings for Allegra. Made up in London by local jewellers, these were inspired by old love rings, with flaming enamel hearts held by golden hands in a cloud of smoke of diamond sparks. I am intrigued by the whole vocabulary of symbols and emblems of alchemy, love and religion that was so important throughout the Renaissance and has remained so up to the modern era. Images like these have a strength even today that fascinates me.

I spent a lot of time in Jaipur, making some first pieces of furniture in the attic of a firm of jewellers – old family friends who happened to have some talented carpenters working above the shop. Jaipur is India's jewellery capital, peopled by Jain families brought to the city by Sawai Jai Singh I, the great maharajah who founded this idyllic place in the late seventeenth century. While the carpenters worked, I would slip down to the courtyard of the shop and sit with the goldsmith as he drew out gold wires by hand, then cut, bent and soldered them into my designs.

There I made a small collection of jewellery designs, many of the pieces inspired by traditional work I saw in museums and books. A

number had eyes as their central motif: rings with small paintings of eyes set under rock crystal in a gold mount, like an eighteenth-century mourning ring crossed with something southern to ward off the evil eye; a necklace with an eye miniature under crystal and plaques of 'Suleimanie' agate, a chic hard stone, black with white markings. The stones used were minimal but interesting, such as old Burmese spinels glowing with deep pinks and reds, and coral, not in the form of polished beads or carvings, but rather in small branches, like minute red trees or antlers.

Coral has a great romance attached to it because of its talisman attributes, appreciated as much today as in the Renaissance, when a silver-mounted pendant of coral would be included in every painting of a baby. One of the most magical places in the world is Schloss Ambras, Innsbruck, where there survives a Wunderkammer, or room of marvels, a miniature museum of curiosities assembled in the 1560s by Archduke Ferdinand of the Tyrol. There is case after case of coral objects, including several large tableaux of the Crucifixion, with tiny, carved coral figures and trees formed by large, natural coral branches.

Two necklaces of my design, opposite, one of flexible gold wire with tiny ruby fish playing in a net, the other a heavy gold band, onto which are clipped pendants of rock crystal and coral. The crystal shapes are derived from **Neapolitan good-luck charms. The coral is simply left as branches. Two inspirational pieces, above: a bronze-age Irish 'Lunula', top, and a Romanesque segmented necklace with sapphires.**

klismos chair

On this page, three historical images of the Klismos chair including, far left, the Stela of Hegeso, circa 430BC. These clearly show the shallow-curved back board of classical times which I reproduced in my version, opposite. How the Greeks made the design leap to curved legs, while all earlier chairs were rigidly straight, remains obscure. One of my sketches, below.

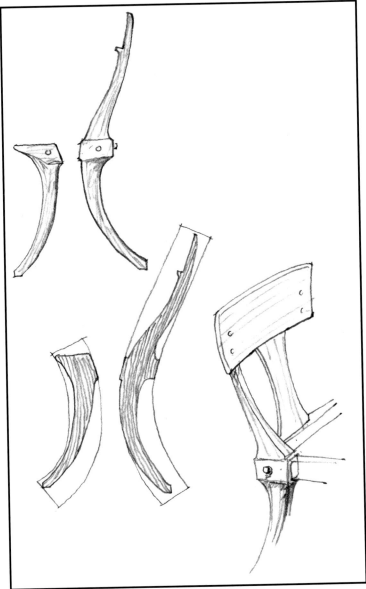

The first thing that truly inspired me to make furniture was not, as it might have been, the fact that I grew up surrounded by beautiful examples, with a father who was constantly telling me the history of everything we saw. This certainly fuelled my interest, maybe even created it. The first real spark came at architecture school when I came across a book on furniture of the ancient world. Among the illustrations were a series of drawings of ancient furniture, including a Greek Klismos chair of around 430BC.

The drawing had been made by the author in the 1920s, following a study of every painted and carved representation of Klismoi, the typical 'easy chair' of the Greeks. Once you start to look for these chairs on the painted pottery of the era, you see them everywhere. The chair's pronounced curves made it comfortable and easy to use, but also a delight to paint, and the pot-painters of Athens and the Greek colonies depicted them in every possible use and situation, from honouring gods and heroes to scenes from everyday life, where carpenters and painters are shown at work seated on Klismoi.

Because of these vivid representations, the chair was one of the key pieces of classical furniture to be reproduced from the eighteenth century onwards as part of the wild craze for all things classical that followed the new fad for the Grand Tour among the nobility of Britain, France and northern Europe. The Klismos was always made, however, in mongrel versions that included Roman era changes, chiefly an exaggeratedly deep curved back. For the most part, its features and parts were grafted on to other designs, its legs becoming the 'sabre' legs of Regency furniture, and so on.

Working with traditional carpenters in India, I eventually succeeded in making a Klismos pretty much as it had been in Athens in 430BC. The size is rather smaller, since we have dispensed with the cushions, foot stools and blanket thrown over the back that the Greeks would have had. Foot stools were essential for the same reason that the chair legs were so curved and their tables were three-legged: Greek houses of the period had rough clay floors. Three legs will always settle. The Klismos legs, with their deep curves, flex enough to settle on a rough surface, which is perhaps the original function behind the form.

thar armchair

Having made the Klismos, I started
to design a collection of furniture
that would work well with it and in
our own decorating style. I also
wanted to make pieces that would
fill a gap that I had noticed in the
market for hand-made, beautiful
furniture that was useful and
comfortable, and that blended
happily with furniture and interiors
of a wide range of styles and eras.
So much modern furniture is so
unforgivingly modern, often
uncomfortable, and so shiny and
new it repels any object of any
greater age, while much 'traditional'
furniture is made up of poor
quality reproductions lacking the
intrinsic beauty of original pieces.

The collection included some
pieces that I knew from our
decorating work were not
available, and would be useful: an
X-frame stool with a leather
cushion, which could serve as a
coffee table and as extra seating
when required, and a bedside table
with a drawer and a shelf below
for storing books and magazines.
I wanted a tall, sculptural piece,
and designed an étagère with six
shelves which could also be broken
down into three stacking tables.
The same thinking lay behind the
rest of the collection, which set
out to identify needs and to
attempt to fill them with
something useful and beautiful.

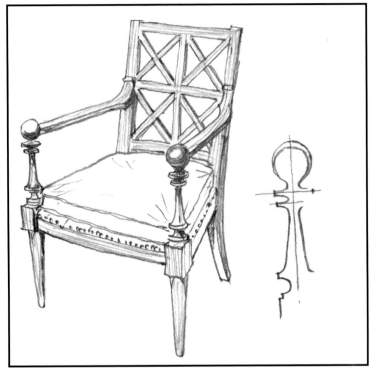

Good dining chairs are not easy to find. The choice is restricted to all-upholstered chairs, which tend to be heavy and uncomfortable, and are a nightmare to keep clean; modern open-frame chairs that are often angular and hard; and reproduction antiques, which are mostly terrible. I had always loved chairs of the French Directoire period of the 1790s, and made two designs very loosely based on these models, but with new motifs that I felt lent a contemporary edge to the designs. The new elements were inspired by a mixture of sources and factors: African tribal art, cubist Czech furniture, and above all the desire to create something new and handmade.

I carefully measured some eighteenth-century chairs and modelled the sizes and outlines of my new pieces on these. On to these bones of good proportion and comfort I then grafted my own design. I always draw every piece out by hand at full size in order to avoid any problems of interpretation, and find the process of drawing each new piece forms an essential part of its making. Drawing at full-size can become an almost sculptural thing, like carving the form from the paper.

I named one of the chairs 'Sheaf' after an abstracted, square wheatsheaf motif that the carpenters carved as arm supports, with a thin, silhouette version of the same form as the back-board. The motif is sculptural, with a feeling of Brancusi's totems and African carvings. The side chair has a cut-out below the top rail, in the manner of a Directoire original, used for carrying the chair around: this I made in a form something like an eye (see page 136), which gives it a personality all its own.

Above, a *fauteuil d'officier* made in Paris, circa 1790, of stripped-down, classically-inspired simplicity typical of Revolutionary period furniture; it has no arms so that an officer could sit with his sword at his side, rather than uncomfortably in front, but has pommels on which to rest his hands. I used the pommel detail and blended this with a simple, Directoire-style frame and a back following the design of a door that I had sketched from a house in the Thar desert of Northwest India, top, to make my 'Thar' armchair, opposite, in dark teak.

5 9

drum table

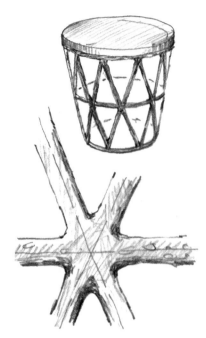

Three African drummers in a lost-wax bronze, among the treasures looted by the British from the palace of The Oba of Benin. My 'Drum' table, opposite, with a hand-forged steel base and a top in tigerwood veneer, was inspired by similar ethnic pieces and by a dynastic Egyptian limestone vase with rope decoration, far right, in the Louvre. This small table is perfect in front of a sofa in a small room, its light, trellis-like base giving it a certain transparency.

I am fascinated by both tribal art and classical art, and if there is ever an opportunity to cross-fertilize these two disparate influences, I always find it irresistible. It does not happen deliberately, but somehow in the quest for new forms and motifs, distant and half-remembered sources will blend together to produce something quite different. For instance, I found that a memory of an African stool became confused with a Roman grille motif and ended up as a small table that looked like a drum. In the end, all that matters is that it makes an attractive little table that fits in many quite different decors.

We have used the same grille motif, a diagonal, triangle-based pattern, on many objects at different scales: on windows and wardrobes, on jewellery and furniture. It makes a perfect security grille as it has no vertical bars and looks unobtrusive and light. In the furniture collection, it appears on the étagère and on the 'Drum' table. On a much larger scale, it forms the roof of the British Museum's spectacular new Great Court. Like so many patterns, once identified it will spring out at you from the most unexpected places.

The collection needed a dining table, and I devised a leg in cast metal with a chiselled texture and a bronze patina that could be fixed to any kind of top. This was very much inspired by the Rateau furniture of the 1920s, although it was simplified to the verge of plainness. The cast leg meant that this piece was very quick to put together and easy to ship. We make tops in any wood and any size, suitable for dining tables, desks or consoles.

Needing a name for my furniture collection, I called it 'Jantar Mantar', after the famous sandstone and marble observatory in Jaipur, built by the same Maharajah Jai Singh who had constructed the city. Having made my first samples in that beautiful place, it seemed only right to remember it in this way. The observatory itself is an extraordinary complex of vast instruments with a powerful, sculptural quality unique to themselves. It has the curious distinction of being the only monument in India that impressed Le Corbusier when he toured the country before starting work on the new city of Chandigarh. Many features of his design can be traced back to the Jantar Mantar.

The most recent addition to my furniture is the 'Bronze

Collection', which combines cast, bronze-patinated metal with exotic woods and upholstery. I had longed to make a chaise longue, or 'Récamier' as they are sometimes known (after the antique-style chaise made by the great ébéniste Jacob for the painter David, and used as a prop in his portrait of Mme Récamier). My chaise has a light metal frame with legs curved in a sweep that recalls the Klismos, an animal-like curve that gives it a look of graceful speed.

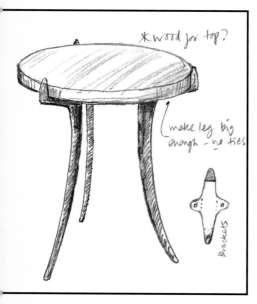

An early sketch for the Sabre table and the finished piece. The painterly grain of the Macassar ebony top works particularly well against the intricate weave of Allegra's 'Sundernagar' kilim. The exotic timber is 'set' like a gemstone in jewellery-style 'claws'. The sweeping curves of the table's legs share, like much of the furniture, aspects of Allegra's formal vocabulary.

sabre table

From the same collection, the 'Sabre' table was inspired by the three-legged round tables of antiquity, seen with cast bronze legs animated by faces, animal feet and garlands in many a Roman wall painting. These were developments of ancient Greek tripod tables, which were themselves descended from Egyptian pieces. And so it goes back. Three legs always ensure stability, as any photographer will tell you, and the tripod construction was doubtless invaluable in ancient houses with rough floors.

With the exception of the occasional archaeological reconstruction, more modern versions of these tables have all been similar to the French Guéridon tables of the eighteenth century, with a light bronze circular frame holding a thin marble top, and a second circle connecting the legs halfway down. These delicate, feminine tables have been a mainstay of decorating forever. I wanted to make something that was more modern and at the same time closer to the classical examples.

The 'Sabre' leg is sufficiently thick, with a large area at the top, that it needs no stabilizing connector below, thus recalling those Roman legs. But here there is no decoration, only the luxury of a hand-cast, hand-finished metal surface, waxed to give it the feel of an art bronze. It has a little upstand – a claw in jewellery terms – to 'hold' the top. The top may be anything, but the standard is macassar ebony, an exotic, highly figured wood that lends the whole piece a precious air.

When it came to materials, I was determined to give a hand-made look and feel to the whole collection. So much new furniture has such a thick coat of lacquer over the wood that it could be melamine or plastic. I wanted to be able to feel the grain of the wood on every piece. Where the frame was of steel, the metal was hammered to give it a hand-forged texture. The result is that every piece in the collection has a curious feel of being neither old nor new, of looking as happy in a stark white modern interior as in a heavily decorated room full of antiques.

All of our furniture, rugs and fabrics share this quality. Any or all of them fit happily in almost any surroundings. Chameleon-like, they can take on the feel of their environment, looking just as modern or traditional as they need to in any situation. They do not jar or shout; they harmonize, without compromising the strength of their design. They are great unifiers in this way, anchoring together whatever disparate elements may surround them.

A fragment of a late Roman wall-painting of an orgy scene yields a fine description of a tripod table with bronze legs and a wooden top. Major museums abound with ancient metal table legs, whose wooden tops are now lost. The Roman urge to decorate meant that most of these were covered with ornament as unrestrained as these revellers, but the basic idea of a cast leg which can attach to any size top with the stability of a tripod was a great inspiration.

combining elements

In many ways, our work consists of combining elements, of putting things together in a dynamic way. We mix ingredients rather like medieval alchemists in a laboratory, each ingredient having some symbolic relevance, the result often being surprising, emotive and stimulating. Our ingredients are far less exotic than the alchemists', employing none of the mysterious essentials of their 'Great Work': no morning dew wrung from white sheets of the purest linen, for instance. Our mixtures are made of far less exciting things, but then ours are a little more useful, a touch more practical.

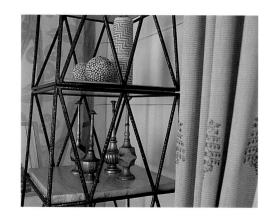

Elements combined: by colour, above, where silver embroidery on the curtains is picked up by silvered rosewater-sprinklers, and by shape, right, where interlocking circles and elipses run through Allegra's 'Spheres' rug, the old Italian marquetry tabletop, and the bowl of pressed courgette slices.

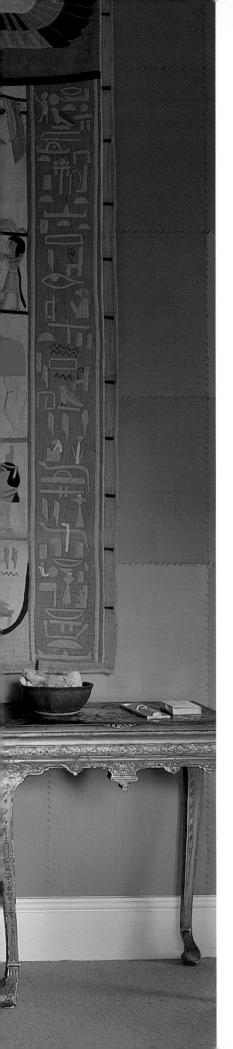

While working with all of the traditional tools of the designer/decorator, with such mundane matters as chairs and tables, rugs and walls, we are also concerned with the more intangible qualities associated with all objects: their style, colour, texture, pattern and form. Much of our work relies on plays of contrast between the ingredients, contrasts which we feel lend a certain strength and edge to a room. It is important not to over-stress the contrasts, however: the elements must be sympathetic to each other, able to meld together rather than fight. Explosions which are too obvious date quickly and tire the eyes.

Always try to look for a unifying quality and for a contrasting one, thus setting up a dynamic that gives energy and interest to the interior. It is this dynamic, this jostling alternation of similarity and difference, this contrast of partners, that recalls the ancient alchemical preoccupation with opposing elements that join and fuse together: sun and moon, man and woman, day and night.

The contrast of historical eras in our own rooms in Oxfordshire: a 1960 Italian chair, an English 1720 gilt table and a 1920 Egyptian wall hanging combine beautifully through their related colouring, shared by my adaptation of the Greek Klismos chairs in the kitchen. The kitchen floor of striped cherry and walnut raises ordinary veneered wood to a new level.

something unexpected

Our London living room is crammed with little surprises, odd pieces that play on each other and gel into a coherent whole. A vermilion feather headdress from Cameroon punches a hole in one wall, right, anchoring all the other red touches and highlights, while a side table, above, holds Jaisalmeri lacquered opium boxes, a Japanese lucky animal and a modern Spanish chrome lamp below a painting by James Brown.

Allegra and I have very few rules in what we do, and certainly none that can never be broken. However, if pushed, this might be the one rule: include something unexpected. The saddest quality in any interior is predictability. Nothing is worse than a safe, dull design, the precise definition of which might change every few years with the whims of fashion, but the quality remains the same. At the time of writing the look is beige on beige with vaguely 1940s furniture, no patterns and the odd ethnic accessory. Safe and dull, it's the little black dress of decoration. It's the look of a thousand smart hotels across the planet. It's boring.

Then there is the other extreme. There is really no need for humour in decoration, no need for wild excess. There can be a place for both, of course, and a very small number of people can create beautiful interiors with them, but on the whole they work better in nightclubs than in homes – environments for living rather than partying. A few brilliant artistic souls have created their own houses with humour and excess

of every kind, such as the late Tony Duquette in California, the Prince Regent in Brighton or Stephen Tennant in Wiltshire, but their lifestyles tended to be more like extended nightclub evenings, and rarely involved families.

Between the two poles of dullness and outrage, there is a whole sphere in which to play, discovering new forms and styles. The unexpected is never hard to find, though the right degree of unexpectedness needs careful judgement. The ideal is to push the barriers slightly, to add elements that are not bizarre but merely surprising. No explosions, no dramatic gestures that will age before their time. Nothing is more dated than a dated interior. A fashion outfit will almost always look interesting, whatever its vintage, but a room with a design that lacks subtlety can become sad and dreary within a few years.

The unexpected can be very mild. Faced with a dark London basement bedroom with no real garden view, we pasted pages from a book of botanical illustrations (a reproduction of a sixteenth-

century Italian herbal) on to faded sage green walls. We then added warm carpeting in a pale tartan design in the same faded greens and pinks as the herbal. The tartan provides the clashing element, the colours unifying. The whole thing lightens and freshens the room, making it a delight to sleep in. If the botanical pictures were framed and the carpet a delicate floral design, the effect would be sad and predictable instead.

In our own house in London, we place pictures and objects that are unfamiliar next to each other, with results that enhance each. Allegra hung a bright red feather headdress from Cameroon in West Africa over a delicate Louis XVI giltwood sofa, beneath a drawing by Anish Kapoor. The drawing features a tiny white circle in the centre of an indigo field, and the red circle of the headdress echoes this, but it is a dramatic element on the wall. The softness and delicacy of the feathers calm their vivid colour and their texture contrasts well with the moulded rail of the sofa below, and with the smooth gilded surface of the picture frame above.

The staircase of the same house is a typically narrow, cramped London stair. When we arrived, it had utterly predictable straight wooden banisters painted white, which made it sad and dull. Life in these houses revolves around the stair as you inevitably have to change floor in order to

cook, eat or sleep. As well as being the hub of the house, the stair is seen from many of the rooms. It is essential to get it right, to give it variety and interest, but also to tie the space together so that it acts as a unifying element in the house.

The first thing we did was to strip out the wooden banisters and call Tom Dixon, a brilliant designer of very modern furniture (who has since revolutionized the UK high street chain Habitat). Tom created nickel-plated steel banisters with playful, children's block motifs cut from thick chunks of steel and welded to thin bars. The motifs repeat once on each short flight, giving both variety and repetition throughout the house, making each flight amusing and fun. Besides which, our children adore it.

We then designed a special wallpaper, combining an alchemical motif of a dove diving into a bottle after the sun and moon with a maze, our initials and the date; all set on a ground of smaller, repeating pattern. The effect of the paper is to pull the different floors of the house together by linking them, by means of the very large repeat of the big motifs, while effectively hiding any marks and stains with the smaller repeating pattern. The combination of modern, abstract forms in the banisters and more traditional ones in the paper lends a certain edge to the space, relieving it of the boring quality of so many narrow stairs. It is without doubt

an unexpected combination, but a very successful one.

Something unexpected is vital. There is nothing like something out of place to give a sense of place to a room, so long as it has some connection with the rest of the contents. At the same time, disparate elements simply thrown together without rhyme or reason, a grab-bag of assorted unrelated pieces, motifs, patterns or colours, united simply by their location, will give a genuine feeling of confusion to any interior. It is only by setting up some kind of principle – of colour, pattern, style – that you are able to inject the surprise elements that will keep the room young and retain your interest.

The stairs in this London house, opposite, had traditional, straight wood banisters, white-painted and dull, which we removed in favour of these nickel-plated steel forms created by Tom Dixon. The contrast of materials between the gleaming nickel metal and the aged, warm oak parquet floor gives this narrow, dark hallway a fresh excitement. The green of our wallpaper, above, sets the theme for a thick glass top with 1950s green glass from Venini.

historical continuity

In a bedroom designed to wake one in southern warmth on the dullest of grey, English mornings, one of my tougher-looking female ancestors is brought up-to-date by discarding her frame and hanging above a table and lamp made from Indian Shesham wood, and a shade in Allegra's 'Tree of Life' fabric. The detail, above, shows the gold silk *bagh* embroidery from the Punjab, mounted as a blind.

One thing we never do is combine elements by date. We don't put eighteenth-century things only with each other, or collect 1860s glass paperweights and mass them together, or hang a seventeenth-century flower picture over a Louis XIV table of the same date, or a Damien Hirst dot painting over a modern nickel-plated chair. There is something so exciting and enriching about the contrast between different eras, which gives a sense of the layering of history, whereas grouping objects of their own time together gives a sterile, closed quality, like a bad costume drama. Period rooms, of whatever era, tend to be deadening and frigid and are best left in museums.

That is not to say that it is impossible to make a stylish room with furnishings of just one period. Personally, we find it uninteresting: we enjoy the stimulation of contrast too much. I also find that over-restored interiors, like some historic houses and museums, lose all of the charm and life they once had when some things were left to accident. There is a dreadfully cloying quality that can arrive with

restoration. It is the odd quirks and accidents, the visible repairs, the mis-matched paint or fabric, the personal touches that give a room life. If these are all purged, so is the life of the space.

The excitement of the historical interiors in our first chapter depends on their being so firmly rooted in the past, but being new and original at the same time. None made any pretence at reproduction, except for the Villa Kerylos, whose technology, piano, heating and shower effectively shattered any ancient Greek illusions. Thus, although most of those rooms were created in their entirety at a single point in time and contained nothing old, the fact that they were based in such a vital manner on earlier styles or periods gives them a sense of historical continuity.

This continuity is the key. While contrasts are exciting, too much of them is glaring and ostentatious, and will date rapidly. You occasionally come across rooms from the 60s that have remained more or less unchanged, with giltwood Louis XV fauteuils in

front of vast abstract canvases, all spotlit, dramatic, shouting at you; often extremely stylish and exciting, they are also terribly dated. They ceased to look truly modern within two or three years. They were never, even in the first place, very comfortable or relaxing. There is something of a challenge in this kind of interior, and challenging things are rarely relaxing.

Of course not everyone wants to have a relaxing interior. Many people want precisely the opposite. They want to impress anyone who enters their rooms. They want to be dramatic, to make a loud statement, to be remembered at all costs. They want that strange atmosphere which first inspired my father to start decorating, a childhood memory of a neighbour's house so perfect that he felt it was bewitched, and that to have moved anything at all might have broken the spell. His own rooms were invariably like this; hard, brittle places which allowed for nothing but the most immaculate of lifestyles.

This was the environment I grew up in, forbidden to touch the objects carefully arranged in 'tablescapes' all around the drawing-room ('Those are Daddy's toys. Yours are upstairs!'). This has given me a slightly less precious attitude to the mess that we all create, and a quite different approach to decorating and design, which Allegra happens to share. We want a cosy, friendly, family atmosphere, we want to see things we love. We want

rooms where you can have a pile of newspapers and magazines strewn on a sofa, where someone might be stretched out in an armchair fast asleep, where children can play in a corner, where the beauty of the interior is not destroyed by such fundamental signs of life.

A gentle sense of historical continuity combined with a sense of adventure in putting things together is a strong element of our work. We revel in juxtapositions that reveal surprising affinities between apparently unrelated things. Some relationship between the objects is important, whether through colour, shape or pattern, as it emphasizes the chronological distance and makes the combination that much more exciting.

A small bedroom in our house in the country, for instance, has a blind made from a 1920s golden silk-embroidered Indian shawl, an English portrait of a lady of 1720, some 1960s glass vases, an Italian 1940s giltwood marble-topped table and some 1990s Donald Baechler monotype animal prints surrounding a large colour photograph of a chair in a Turinese palace in an 1860s frame. They all look very happy together, but each provokes the others in its own way. The portrait was removed from its heavy and ugly frame and now the canvas looks modern and fresh. The photograph frame had heavy Victorian gilding; now painted white, it has a lightness that is perfect with the Baechlers' white frames.

What is it that unites these disparate elements, apart from a bit of white paint? There are a few reds: the lady's dress, the glass vases, the border of the shawl/blind, parts of the Baechler prints, and an Indian Tantric diagram. And there is a lot of gold: the room is painted golden yellow as a defence against the dreary grey of the English sky, the bed is covered and hung with rust and yellow silks, the table's rather Etruscan legs are gilt, and the whole is pulled together by the massive expanse of gold embroidery on the blind which takes up most of one wall. So here the elements are separated by time (and geography), yet united by colour.

At the end of a bed, above, my photograph of a chair at Stupinigi, the exquisite baroque hunting lodge outside Turin, is surrounded by contemporary prints given to our daughter Angelica by the artist, Donald Baechler. These contrasting elements are united by their white frames. A neo-Greek table, opposite, made in Turin in 1950 for Allegra's grandmother, continues the gold theme in the same room.

colour

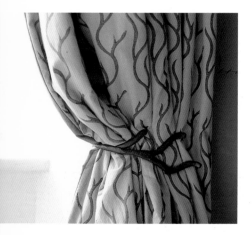

An Indian watercolour, opposite, a present from our friend Munnu Kasliwal, stands on the stippled 'pink sandstone' chimneypiece, against walls painted to look like sewn panels of green leather. The green and pink scheme mimics the colours of the famous 'Pink City' of Jaipur in Rajasthan, where Allegra's fabrics were first sampled. Her 'Tree of Life' curtains, above, are held back by forged tie-backs adapted from the pattern.

That yellow bedroom leads us into the world of colour. We have no firm theories or rules concerning the use of colour. All of us have our own sense of colour and a scheme that we might think of as beautiful, many would find dull and turgid, and others overpowering. Volumes have been written on the subject, therapies concocted around it and philosophies based on it. Goethe devoted a whole section of his work to a theory of colour harmony. We take a rather lighter approach, but colour is a major element in our work and it is certainly one of the keys to our technique of combining elements.

The living room of our own country house has a colour scheme that came about in an odd, subconscious way. We both had the same idea of painting the living room green, not a bright green but a faded, sage grey-green, or rather lots of them, in squares painted to look like green leather panels stitched together. With this we put one of Allegra's first printed fabrics, the 'Tree of Life' on a dirty pink ground. It was a strange combination, but it worked. The pink colour that Allegra had chosen in Jaipur, when printing the first samples of hand-blocked cotton, was perfect with the green.

The next time we visited Jaipur, we realized that the pink was exactly the colour of most of the buildings there (the famous 'Pink City' was painted that colour in 1860 in imitation of the local

sandstone); while our greens echoed other colours used throughout the city. Somehow we had replicated the colour scheme without consciously thinking about it. Allegra then painted an ugly Edwardian mahogany chimneypiece in 'faux' sandstone; we hung some Jain astrological scrolls bought in Jaisalmer, which had the same greens and pinks; and the whole scheme fell into place. There is nothing very Indian about the room: the scrolls are very subtle, and the dominant object is an Egyptian appliqué panel. The decor is like a half-memory of Jaipur, more like a taste-memory than a visual one, and as such it is highly evocative of the atmosphere of that lovely town.

How are the colours used in the room? They are all very subtle, all muddied down so that pink and green sit well together. The other colours are sandy beiges, dark stone greys, rust reds. All this rich, glowing, earthy colour is set off by white skirtings and a huge white cornice, exaggeratedly deep and crisply detailed. The colours are drawn entirely from the green-yellow-red side of the spectrum, mostly of greyish, understated hues. There is not even a hint of blue. These slight hues are quite different from the yellow bedroom, where the wall colour is a powerful, glowing yellow, with sharp accents of bright red on a field of gold: all from the yellow-red side only.

In a small house overlooking Lake Geneva, our clients had a

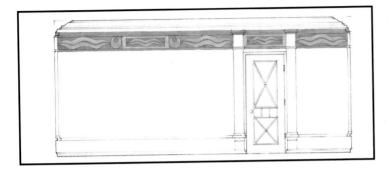

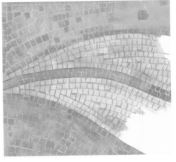

This Swiss house already had floors in local terracotta tiles, which the clients wished to continue in their new living room. We created a frieze running around the new space, painted in imitation mosaic in terracotta and bone colours, and found fabrics that shared this palette, thus making the tiled floor appear central to the scheme. The cut-leather radiator screen also picks up on this colour.

limited budget and a garage to add to their living room. This posed complicated structural and spatial problems, and also a major colour question. As the whole ground floor was already laid with terracotta tiles, we needed to use matching tiles and somehow elevate them from their prosaic reality into a seemingly positive choice. Rather than try to ignore them, we made the scheme around the tiles so that in the end they look special and considered. The walls are a delicate creamy beige, a textured *stucco romano* made by a local craftsman who has worked for us in London too. The fabrics are plays on the theme of cream/pink/terracotta. An ugly bulkhead containing pipework around the top of the new room was disguised by a frieze painted in imitation mosaic in the terracotta colours of the floor tiles. In this way the tiles are made to look central to the decoration of the room.

We adopted an entirely different approach in our London living room. The house is not large and we wanted to introduce a sense of unity, so we resolved to

use subtle changes of one colour throughout, with accents of different colours in different rooms. For the main colour we chose a light, sandy beige that was neutral but warm, warmth being very important in the cold, grey London light. On the stairs this was the ground colour of the wallpaper, printed in a muted green, with other accents in greens and lilac. The window retains Victorian glass of bright green around the edge, which suggested the green accents.

The living room, meanwhile, revolves around pinks and reds against the sandy walls. We had a lot of pieces of Indian embroidery and silk weaves in bright pinks and magenta, and turned these into cushions and tablecloths. We made a new sofa in a dirty, dull pink and a pair of chairs in salmon. The rug is Allegra's 'Spheres' dhurry, whose colouring reflects the overall scheme: a pale beige ground with sweeping red ovals. On the walls is a collection of contemporary drawings and one oil painting, a rather grand portrait of Edward VII with luscious, heavy brushwork; all with red elements. Finally, a red

feather headdress punches a great red hole in the centre of one wall.

The exception was the dining room, where we hung my grandmother's Marion Dorn curtains at the window, and painted the walls in *trompe l'oeil* with dirty pinks, greys and silver suggested by the curtain fabric. This is a well-tried method for finding colour ideas for an interior: focus on one object, picture or fabric as a starting point and develop a scheme from that. Historical sources also offer rich ideas for colour schemes: the idea is not to imitate a historical interior, but rather to copy colours from historical material. Early Renaissance paintings are wonderful sources, as are eighteenth- or nineteenth-century watercolours of interiors, old costumes and textiles.

Some people are happy with an interior like a Fauvist painting, with bright and jazzy colours clashing like mad, while others prefer a minimalist scheme with white everything and no colour at all. We naturally prefer our way, which admittedly is historically proven to the extent that the same kind of thing has been done for millennia; but this is not to say that ours is the only way. As in other aspects of our work we have no firm rules, but we have learned that with strong hues you can only use one third (or less) of the colour spectrum, and at most two thirds with subtler hues. Beyond this, you lose all harmony and comfort and enter an acidic and chaotic world.

materials

A large mirrored cabinet in this breakfast/TV room, fitted with shelving to three of its four walls, gains both luxury and interest from its details. Cast-bronze snake handles on drawers which pull open to reveal CD storage within, and silver-leaf mirrors, which break up the reflections and add a textural interest of their own.

Materials can be hugely exciting. A lot of pretentious stuff is said today about honesty in materials, truth to materials and so on. After five years of architecture school I personally had heard enough on that subject to last a lifetime. On the other hand, there is nothing worse than an excess of 'dishonest' materials, with everything fake or painted 'faux'. Beautiful effects can be achieved with paint, and there are many rooms in this book that include it; but too much of it is very cloying and awkward. The glut of marbling and 'faux bois' from a few years ago is now being swept away by the vogue for minimalist white: both are excessive and uninteresting, but the 'faux' was probably the greater of the two evils.

Similarly, too much veneered wood can be oppressive. Large expanses of shelving, libraries especially, are often much better painted in some kind of stone colour. All the libraries featured in this book are made with painted MDF and plywood, which also has the advantage of being less expensive. Veneer is unnatural and, like 'faux' paintwork, is better in small quantities and carefully designed. New marquetry or inlay is very difficult to get right, and almost all of what is being made now is frankly hideous and cheap looking – but cheap it certainly is not.

Unlike lighting, where the ideal is to have as many different sources and kinds as possible, with materials the ideal is to have as few as possible, so that you can achieve a simplicity and clarity that is otherwise impossible. While this applies to flooring, walling, storage, doors and so on – the hard, fixed items – it is not true for fabrics and furniture. While many people think that you should use only one kind of wood in a room, or only one colour of wood, this is nonsense: ten different woods in the same space will be just as interesting and pretty as ten different colours, provided that they sit happily together.

The materials and colours of floor, walls and so on should be kept to a minimum. A wood floor is best in one colour only. If there is a border, it must be perfectly made, substantial, and following precisely the form of the room, and only where the room itself is a beautiful shape. Too often you see an apologetic little line that shows up every defect of bad architecture that would be better left unemphasized. Patterned stone floors are also very easy to get wrong and nearly all new ones are, sadly, disasters. They can so easily be copied from historical examples, which are almost all wonderful, but they need to be very carefully executed. The safer and better alternative is to opt for a plain floor of simple wood or stone.

Skirting boards (or base boards) are very practical, as anyone with a modern house that lacks them will tell you after a few years of accumulated vacuum cleaner scratches and marks along the bottom of their walls. The minimalist 'shadow gap' in which skirtings are replaced with a small aluminium channel, a 'negative space', is perfect in an art gallery, where walls are re-painted every six months, but hopeless in a house. It also gives none of the

'faux' was probably the greater of the two evils.

Similarly, too much veneered wood can be oppressive. Large expanses of shelving, libraries especially, are often much better painted in some kind of stone colour. All the libraries featured in this book are made with painted MDF and plywood, which also has the advantage of being less expensive. Veneer is unnatural and, like 'faux' paintwork, is better in small quantities and carefully designed. New marquetry or inlay is very difficult to get right, and almost all of what is being made now is frankly hideous and cheap looking – but cheap it certainly is not.

Unlike lighting, where the ideal is to have as many different sources and kinds as possible, with materials the ideal is to have as few as possible, so that you can achieve a simplicity and clarity that is otherwise impossible. While this applies to flooring, walling, storage, doors and so on – the hard, fixed items – it is not true for fabrics and furniture. While many people think that you should use only one kind of wood in a room, or only one colour of wood, this is nonsense: ten different woods in the same space will be just as interesting and pretty as ten different colours, provided that they sit happily together.

The materials and colours of floor, walls and so on should be kept to a minimum. A wood floor is

Our own dining-room chimneypiece, above, and my sketch, right, showing its various elements, thrown together and painted by Allegra in a subtle, pink faux marble that takes its colour, like that of the painted walls, from the curtains, which were my grandmother's from Brook House. The materials are all fake, being painted plaster and wood, except for the central, Victorian plaque of white marble.

Materials can be hugely exciting. A lot of pretentious stuff is said today about honesty in materials, truth to materials and so on. After five years of architecture school I personally had heard enough on that subject to last a lifetime. On the other hand, there is nothing worse than an excess of 'dishonest' materials, with everything fake or painted 'faux'. Beautiful effects can be achieved with paint, and there are many rooms in this book that include it; but too much of it is very cloying and awkward. The glut of marbling and 'faux bois' from a few years ago is now being swept away by the vogue for minimalist white: both are excessive and uninteresting, but the

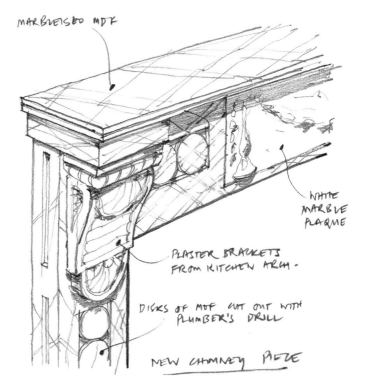

MARBLEISED MDF

WHITE MARBLE PLAQUE

PLASTER BRACKETS FROM KITCHEN ARCH.

DISKS OF MDF CUT OUT WITH PLUMBER'S DRILL

NEW CHIMNEY PIECE

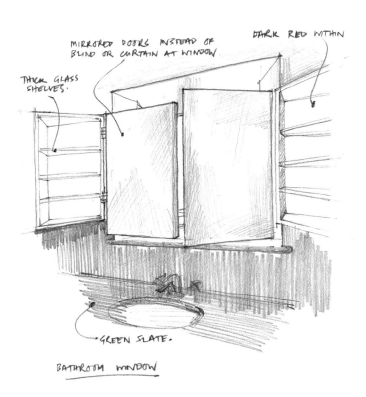

THICK GLASS SHELVES.

MIRRORED DOORS INSTEAD OF BLIND OR CURTAIN AT WINDOW.

DARK RED WITHIN

GREEN SLATE.

BATHROOM WINDOW

stones once inlaid the intricate motifs in the marble pools and columns. There is still something to be gained from small amounts of precious material, for example using silver leaf behind glass in place of ordinary mirror. This produces a wonderful, diffuse reflection, a kind of textured reflection, as if looking through a dream. For a scheme in Geneva, we painted a faux-mosaic frieze around the top of a room, and here, without the expense or complication of real mosaic, we introduced a little slice of luxury that adds immeasurably to the feel of the finished room.

In our own London house, we needed a chimneypiece for the dining room since the hearth had been blocked up by a previous tenant. We looked, but all the pieces we liked were hideously expensive. In the end, I designed something that we made ourselves from MDF, with a detail of flat roundels in recesses copied from an 1840s house we'd seen in beautiful Savannah, Georgia. The roundels were also cut from thin MDF using a plumber's drill-saw intended for making holes for pipes. We incorporated two pretty plaster brackets that we found in the house, and a small Victorian marble plaque that my father gave us. Allegra created such a convincing marble effect on the MDF that people have to touch it in order to be persuaded that it is not real.

Almost everything that Allegra and I use in our work is hand-made, and we always stress this aspect of the materials that we use in interiors, and those that we make things from. The tiny imperfections that show each piece is an individual creation, that a pair of chairs are, like human twins, very slightly different, or that a rug's hand-dyed wool gives it a watercolour-like striated look, similar to the original drawing: these are essential parts of the work, that separate it from the machine-made, mass-produced homogeneity that, increasingly, surrounds us all.

A country bathroom window, set in immensely thick, old chalk walls, has no curtains or blind, which would have been fussy and impractical, but instead cabinets whose doors, mirrored on both sides, swing open to shield the window. The cabinets are wedge-shaped, so the mirrors, when closed, give a three-quarters view like an old dressing table mirror. Reflected is a painting by Langlands & Bell.

texture

The decoration of this London living room centres on Allegra's 'Sundernagar' kilim and one of my Jantar Mantar 'Bronze-X' ottomans covered in parchment-coloured leather. The even, subtle colour scheme of sand and faded pinks is given strength and interest by the textural contrasts of Giovanni Lombardo's rough plastered walls, the introduction of different fabrics (prints, weaves and embroideries) and the wonderfully sensual moss fringe edging the sofa.

The interest of a suede handrail on a rough metal balustrade or of a waxed bronze snake on a painted door is largely textural. Texture is by no means as important as other qualities in our work, but it is there all the same. It is one of those qualities whose contrasts or similarities we play on. When choosing fabrics for a room, we work as much with texture as with colour and pattern. As described earlier, we often limit ourselves to a tiny range of colour, a mere quarter or third of the spectrum, and this means that we rely heavily on texture and pattern for variety. In these small details lies the making of the room, with great opportunities for enjoyable and interesting contrasts.

A living room in North London, for instance, had little interest and a north-facing window. Our clients owned a beautiful *susani*, a traditional Uzbek tent-hanging embroidered with chain stitch on a magenta ground, and some delicate photographs of atmospheric interiors in faded colours. From these we devised a colour scheme of sandy yellows,

faded pinks and off-white. The *susani* was mounted on cloth as a Roman blind. One sofa we covered in a faded 'tea-stained' pink chintz of big blowsy roses, the print so subtle it was almost not there, and another in a tight, rough chenille weave in a dark salmon colour.

To add a subtle excitement to this slightly bland scheme, we trimmed the tea-chintz sofa with a cream heavy moss fringe, and made a collection of cushions using a variety of antique Indian silk weaves and embroideries, some shiny and smooth, others heavily textured. The moss fringe is a terribly old-fashioned thing, having been the height of chic with the work of the famous London decorator Syrie Maugham in 1930, but it remains a delight to run your fingers through, the ultimate in textured decoration, to my mind.

Other interesting textures can be achieved by using the backs of woven fabrics. This is not a sensible thing to do, of course, since the loose threads on the back will unravel or tear before long; but on small cushions that get little wear, it can offer a sense of heavy and

The loggia of a Turin villa which
we transformed from a fussy,
dull room with parquet floor and
mean bookcases into this fresh,
balcony-like space. The local
'Bargellino' stone floor provides
huge textural interest and
separates the loggia from the
adjacent parquet-floored living
rooms. The simple, outside flavour
is continued with the chic but
plain furniture, all found in the
house and painted to fit the
room. Yellow glass set in the top
panes of my new windows fights
the northern, grey light, and the
windows are studded with
decorative rivets to link them to
the 1910 origins of the house.

surprising texture. The reverse sides of some silk weaves are wonderful used in this way, as even an obvious pattern will become more subtle, strange and, in the end, interesting. I particularly enjoy doing this with gauzy old sari silks that we find in little dress shops in Delhi, but it works with many different fabrics.

In Turin, we decorated a house originally built by an engineer in 1909, a great pompous villa that had steadily increased in ugliness as each generation added their own mistakes. The low point was a little enclosed veranda or loggia, floored in delicate parquet and featuring awkward, low bookshelves under double-glazed windows that contained plastic venetian blinds trapped between the panes of glass. An uglier room I never saw.

The outsides of the house and the adjoining garage were painted with a very smart blockwork pattern, linear and crisp. This we imitated on the walls of the loggia, to emphasize its exterior nature. To separate it from the drawing-rooms next door, we took up the dreadful parquet and laid in its place a floor of rough grey and yellow local stone. The contractor wanted to polish the stone, a refinement he believed essential for domestic use, but we insisted on its being left rough, partly to give an exterior feel and partly to contrast with the painted, stylized 'stonework' walls. The two colours are often used in a diamond pattern but we separated them with the centre of the floor in

yellow surrounded by a grey border abutting the original beautifully carved doorcases. These were in a depressing dark mahogany, but when painted a dark grey stone colour, the contrast of texture with the rough floor was marvellous.

When finished, the house was filled with an extraordinary collection of furniture, pictures and objects amassed by our client over a number of years, including a lot of carpets of varying quality and beauty. In order to use a number of these while avoiding dotting the floors with many small rugs, which often looks makeshift and messy, we laid several on tables in the manner of the sixteenth and seventeenth centuries. 'Table-carpets' were sometimes specially made, but more often fine carpets were draped over tables, as may be seen in countless portraits of the period.

What was quite ordinary 400 years ago is now exotic, and a carpet on a table has a splendidly rich textural impact. The table should be made to fit the carpet so that it falls precisely to the floor; unseen, it can be made from plywood. The textural effect is similar to cushions made from cut-up kilims. In the same way, we took a damaged rug from our dhurry collection and covered a pair of white-painted antique French chairs. The feel of the coarse cotton weave against the smooth white painted wood is wonderful. The over-scaled pattern of the rug is also intriguing when cut into small fragments.

pattern

A small guest bedroom in London, opposite, is brought to life with a battery of patterns. The walls were painted by Mario Penati with our adaptation of an old Turkish tulip design taken from a kaftan in the Sultan's wardrobe in the Topkapi Palace, Istanbul. The bed is piled with cushions in a variety of materials and designs, mostly Indian. The form of Allegra's watercolour of a drop picks up the centre of the Turkish tulip. Detail of an Uzbek *susani* embroidery used as a blind, above.

Pattern is hugely important in our work. One of the first things that strikes most people about our rooms is the abundance of patterns. There are Allegra's fabric patterns and rugs; other fabrics and papers; painted walls with patterns stencilled on as flat, repeat patterns or added in *trompe l'oeil* perspective as three-dimensional patterns; embroidered cushions and hangings; and the patterns in many of the artworks that we hang and on many of the antiques and objects that we use.

There is, of course, no such thing as a new pattern; every conceivable, possible pattern already exists in some form or other, either in the natural world or in some historic example. This is one of the joys of using patterns; every form links to another set or family of forms, every line leads to some other half-remembered design. Patterns can be calming or enervating, sophisticated or primitive, crystalline, wavelike or mechanical. Pattern is decorative but also very practical as it will always hide marks and stains: a patterned fabric will last three or

four times longer than a plain one, while a patterned wallpaper on a staircase will absorb all of those inevitable scratches and marks of everyday wear and tear.

The majority of design today uses pattern in a very closed way, using only similar motifs from the same period in sparing fashion, or not at all, preferring blank minimalism. You will find rooms of chintz on chintz on *toile de Jouy*; rooms of Eames-style mid-century modern graphic designs and nothing else; rooms of neo-classical stripes and waistcoat silks; rooms with endless textured weaves in close colour combinations; and countless rooms where the owner or designer, believing that one pattern is all that a room can take, has used the same fabric on a sofa and the curtains and left everything else plain.

A quick look at historical sources speaks volumes about people's love for pattern through the ages and across the globe. We tend to view the history of decoration from a modern perspective which suggests that any historical moment was

impeccably homogenous, with Victorian rooms containing only Victoriana, and so on. In fact, any contemporary drawing or painting of an interior will show just how mixed and interesting these rooms often really were. Look at any era, and you will find layer upon layer of imagery, pattern and period; it is only today that many people seem frightened of making mistakes, and hence play it safe and bland.

Allegra and I love to pile pattern onto pattern, while taking care to avoid the crowded, overwhelming effect this can produce. The key is a little discipline and an eye for the kind of combination that will dance just enough to amuse, avoiding both the bland and the exaggeratedly jazzy. For instance, we have hung a framed fragment of an Egyptian Coptic tunic from around AD450 over a sofa covered in a brand new Indian woven cotton to fascinating effect, as the sofa's striped design of running animals echoed the colour and style of the tunic border of fifteen centuries earlier.

We often mix fabrics of similar colour but with very different

patterns, perhaps putting a soft, faded chintz design of pink roses on sandy linen with a couple of Allegra's sharp and deliberate printed cottons, with slightly ethnic forms recalling their first printing by wood blocks in India. Allegra's patterns have a vocabulary of their own, one that shares elements with many sources but has a roundness to it that includes large and small motifs, stripes and wavy designs. They share a simplicity and directness that is the perfect foil for the many sophisticated, subtle designs such as that old chintz.

We use printed, woven or embroidered patterns on fabrics for upholstery or curtains; embroidered patterns on hangings used on walls in place of pictures; woven patterns as rugs on the floor; patterns worked in wood furniture; in wallpaper and painted or stencilled onto the wall. The effect could be cloying and oppressive, but we are careful to vary the scale of the designs, to use few big-scale patterns, to leave large areas of plain surface, to link the varied patterns through similar tones and colours, or to vary the similar patterns with different tones or colours.

Occasionally we find one motif that lends itself to different elements in a room, such as a star copied from the existing mosaic floor of a huge staircase hall in Italy and painted, at a greatly increased scale, on its walls, as described on the following page. We might use an element from a painting like the great American decorator Billy Baldwin, who had part of a Matisse drawing screenprinted, in repeat and with black and white reversed, onto the cover of the sofa below the real framed drawing. You can find a fabric that shares one motif, one shape with a rug, and so on.

Used in this way, patterns in our interiors begin to tell a story; a story in which the abstract or figurative forms of the design are both characters and vocabulary, and which appears to have a sense to it, rather than being a confused mass of unrelated elements. The same is true of every aspect of a room's design; related forms, colours and textures will lend a coherence to the space and appear part of the 'story'. And like all good stories, it needs a little surprise, a little of the unexpected and a lot of love.

Are there rules or systems that can be applied to patterns? Not really, as it's far too subjective a matter for that sort of treatment, but perhaps a possible guide might be to use either similar patterns in different colours, or very different patterns in similar colours. Or a form or shape from one pattern might be picked up in another entirely different design, and so link the two. It is very important to vary the scale of different patterns used together, to have huge, medium and small repeats all in one room, as this somehow expands the space. Confining patterns to small geometric repeats will immediately suggest a commercial airliner or boardroom, while big repeats used exclusively become claustrophobic and confusing.

A entire encyclopaedia of uses for patterns, as for colour, is to be found in paintings of all eras and these often depict adventurous combinations that work extremely well. Rich sources for patterns are the great ethnographical museums, such as the extraordinary Field Museum in Chicago which is a treasure trove of motifs and books on the subject. The use of pattern in 'primitive' societies is especially rich and exciting, partly because the motifs are always hand-drawn, partly because they are usually confined to a palette of one or two colours, white and earth tones, which always looks tremendously chic. The shapes and markings used in patterns in many of these societies have a complex symbolism that is fascinating to discover, although our own use of them purges them of any significance other than the purely aesthetic.

The repetitive motifs of an Indian city view, above left, are picked up by Allegra's 'Jaipur' fabric on the sofa, while her abstracted 'Waterlily' fabric contrasts interestingly with the naturalism of an Osborne & Little paper, right. Patterns can be picked from, like the old Indian design on dining room curtains, opposite, from which one flower was taken, enlarged greatly, and painted onto the cotton-upholstered backs of inexpensive dining chairs to create a hugely stylish room on a limited budget. Far left, a detail of an appliqué carnation motif made with striped handloom silk on natural linen.

form and shape

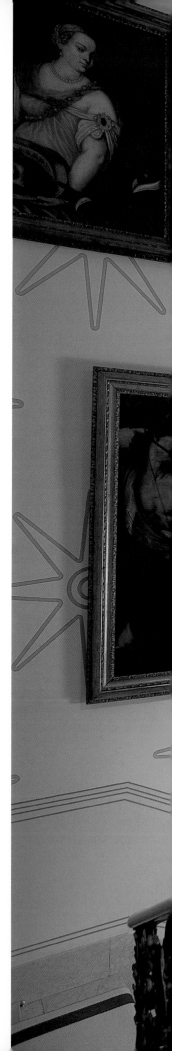

A star pattern, opposite, pulls together this overwhelming and dramatic entrance hall in Italy, simplifying, modernizing and making the space more intimate. The elaborate architectural ornament was originally painted in an elaborate Beaux-Arts colour scheme with lots of gold, all of which we removed, leaving a grey colour similar to the local stone. The star motif, taken from the original mosaic floor and increased vastly in scale for the walls, reappears in the form of a new, steel lantern and in the grey fabric, above, on an old Genoese sofa.

Patterns consist of linked or related shapes, but we can make connections between the various elements that make up an interior on another level: through the stepped-back level of simple shapes or forms themselves. Shapes within patterns, shapes within pictures or objects, shapes of objects or furniture themselves, these may be subtle or startlingly obvious. They often occur subconsciously, and only when an interior is finished will we notice, for instance, that triangular-shaped table tops link graphically to the triangles formed by the metal trellis of another table

base. At other times they may be studiedly deliberate, in which case they must be carried out with care and subtlety, in order not to seem heavy-handed and obvious.

In a house in Italy with an exaggeratedly large entrance hall and staircase, we needed to pull the space together, to shrink it and make it manageable, lending it a human scale that it lacked. It has a beautiful mosaic floor with a complicated design containing one simple element – a slender, eight-pointed star – dating from the early years of the twentieth century. This I enlarged it to make a star about a metre in diameter. The walls were then carefully divided and the stars painted by hand to align perfectly in each corner. We then found two fabrics with similar star motifs, covered the furniture with one and made a great curtain with another.

The space was dark and depressing when I found it, and needed light more than anything. A single huge window faced north towards a steep hill so that the little light that entered was cold and grey. The strong yellow colour

we chose for the star pattern improved things, but there was still the question of where to put lighting. A dramatic solution would make this space the focus of the house, while breaking it up a little so that it would seem less cavernous. In the end, we made a huge new hanging lantern out of steel, an eight-pointed star in plan, with 24 spotlights that could be adjusted to pick out details of the architecture and the vast paintings on the walls. Thus the star shape holds the whole space together and gives it a focus.

In our own bedroom in London the bed is crowned with a 'baldaquin' of curtains hanging from a central, circular pelmet; the pelmet is made up of triangular forms, alternately bordered and plain, a design I adapted from a Parisian window treatment dating from 1810. To make the large wardrobe facing the bed in this small room less obtrusive, I designed the front of it with mirrored doors and with glazing bars on the mirror to lighten the piece. The glazing bars are diagonal, forming one of my favourite trellis patterns, made of large triangles that echo the triangles of the bed corona. Here again, shapes speak to each other and give a sense that they belong.

The key to many a successful interior lies in its details. Without having to go to the extravagant lengths of the astounding Armand Albert Rateau, who even made

exquisitely fine keys for every door in every project, choosing the right details will give a room a real sense of completeness. You may happen upon the perfect curtain tie-backs, for instance, or you may choose to have them specially made, so providing that extra something that makes all the difference. The curtains in our own country living room, made in Allegra's 'Tree of Life' fabric design, are held by tie-backs created by a local blacksmith in forged iron, their forms echoing the pattern of the fabric.

Linking elements by shape or by form does not necessarily entail making things specially. It can also be achieved simply by putting together objects and furniture that are connected by a common shape, thus pulling the space together. In our London home, standing on Allegra's 'Spheres' dhurry, we have a beautiful eighteenth-century Italian marquetry table, on which sits a fragile bowl made from compressed and dried courgette slices (an unusual present from a favourite cousin). These three objects share one thing: each has a pattern of overlapping ovals. The rug does it with woven lines; the table with a repeating pattern of overlapping circles in three different colours of wood inlay; and the bowl, with its layers of translucent, dried vegetable.

Again in London, one of our clients had a large circular table

that had been quite happy in her old, square dining room, but which now had to move to one end of a new, large living room. This was a messy sort of rectangle, with enormous bi-folding double doors opening into the other end and a pair of terrible plaster columns forming an awkward shallow alcove with a second door into the other end of the room. In order to give clarity to the space, and lend a sense of belonging to the round table, we devised a curved partition wall that replaced the columns and formed a true alcove whose curve was drawn from the centre of the table. As a bonus, the second, pointless door

In our living room, above, triangular end tables flank the sofa, their angled sides allowing access to the room. Our bedroom, opposite, is dominated by the huge bed, its size disguised by the baldaquin fixed to the ceiling, from which hang curtains in a fabric adapted from an old Fortuny design. At the foot of the bed, a low chest of my design with inset panels and straps of tan leather stands on Allegra's 'Twig' dhurry. The framed photograph by the Douglas Brothers hangs over a small bookcase neatly filled with old Italian novels with white spines.

The large curved wall we built to add focus and a much-needed sense of place to a London client's dining room, with my sketches of it before and after, indicating the effect to the client. The wall was decorated with squares of subtly different tones of parchment, honey and bone, in imitation of Jean-Michel Frank's famous parchment-walled salons of the 30s. This gives it an added presence, belying its plasterboard construction. The wall's gentle sweeping curve is echoed in that of the wide, shallow arch that frames it, the whole composition providing both a dramatic entrance to the living room beyond and a perfect solution to the dining room itself.

behind the curve became a valuable extra cupboard.

This is another way in which shapes can pull an interior together. A carefully placed and composed curve will work wonders in providing a focus, a sense of place, an emphasis within the larger composition, either in plan or in elevation (where a vaulted ceiling serves the same purpose). The effect depends to some extent on symmetry: where a symmetrically centred curve will enhance most designs, an asymmetrical one will confuse and distract. Clever uses of such curves are found everywhere in classical architecture, ranging from the simplest to the most complex example; by mentally stripping

them of all their ornamentation, you can see what can be used to your own advantage.

The work that Allegra and I do is, in essence, a matter of combining elements. As well as combining different, unrelated historical and cultural sources in our work, we bring to it our own quite different visions and backgrounds, somehow synthesizing these into a whole that we feel has a coherence and a unity. The elements we use are generally the simplest things: there is no rarefied high theory or specialist knowledge used here, just an enthusiastic interest in the past and in the world around us, spiced with a little imagination and a lot of experimentation.

rooms for living

Here we have selected eight of our interiors, eight homes that presented us with a variety of problems, all very different. Two are our own houses, the others belong to clients. These clients vary greatly

in every respect except one: they all liked something that we had already done, and trusted us to help them make a better and more beautiful home than they might have been able to create by themselves. Most were keen to avoid a 'decorated' look, and wanted us to weave our personal style around their own possessions and ways of living.

In Italy, I designed a scheme of architectural paintwork for a small bathroom that celebrates the sequence of tiny spaces with a faux-pine trelliswork inspired by eighteenth-century porcelain seen in a Lausanne museum. The wall-lights were given new parchment shades, a local tradition.

This is the key to working with clients, and it is what we value most about such work. It is never very interesting to create in a vacuum, and nothing is more pointless than making interiors that fail to express their owners' personalities. There are some decorated houses whose owners almost need a guidebook to steer them around, with an atmosphere more like a chic hotel than a home. One of the chief joys of making things for people is their pleasure in the finished product, and few will enjoy a house that does not feel like home.

The rooms on the following pages have new elements combined into them, elements specific to each project: specific to the clients, to their possessions and tastes, to the location and to the particular problems presented by each. Our solutions are sometimes mundane, sometimes surprising. We try hard not to make rooms that are memorable above all else, that are dramatic and impressive at the expense of comfort or ease. Instead, these are all consciously, deliberately and, we hope, successfully, rooms for living.

Our dining room: a scheme I designed and Allegra painted with Mario Penati. Billowing curtains in a Turkish cintamani design reveal a grey city beyond, with silvered vitrines holding models of eighteenth-century houses. The table extends to seat 14 with my Klismos chairs. On the chimneypiece, Angelica and Allegra painted by Julia Condon.

a house near sloane square

This is our own fairly ordinary house in a street off the King's Road in London. The house was built around 1850 and is typical of medium-sized London houses of the date, with two rooms on each floor, and a stair projecting slightly from the back of the house. These houses are so dominated by the stair that it is a crucial element. We are fortunate that ours projects as it does, allowing a small landing at each turn. The landings make all the difference in that they give enough space for a piece of furniture and a picture, making the journey up and down the stair a little less dull.

When we first saw the house it had every conceivable thing wrong with it, from the L-shaped living room to the brass 'Louis XV' light fittings throughout. There was beige wall-to-wall carpet right through the house, apart from the hall which had a marble-tile-effect plastic floor in colours so hideous I cannot remember them. We had little time to work on the house, as our first baby was due at any moment, and a limited budget, but we were sure from the start that, with just a little work and a few basic changes, it would be perfect for us.

What's wrong with an L-shaped living room? The problem with L-shaped rooms, unless they are very big, is that one end of them is almost always cold, lonely and unlived-in. People naturally congregate in one long space, and the unseen end of the 'L' gets forgotten or abandoned. Architecturally, the sensation is of a box intruding from one corner of a larger space, and this feels claustrophobic and difficult. You can solve the problem with free-standing furniture, a decorative screen for instance, but I was very keen to have a symmetrical, balanced space in the first-floor living room, and to create a new room, a tiny library, in the other end of the 'L'. This would also give us an extra wall for picture-hanging and extra space for bookshelves in the library.

We therefore closed off the end of the room, forming a new doorway that balanced the existing door to the stairs and matched the two long windows overlooking the street. We now had a symmetrical room, and emphasized this fact by making an early Georgian-style box cornice, slightly over-scaled for the room, which considerably increased the apparent height of the space. The existing door into the room was a typical panelled one which, when open, took up precious space on the end wall and intruded into the room. I replaced this with a pair of slender,

glazed doors, much lighter to look at and taking up no space at all, and made a matching pair for the new room.

The tall windows still had their original panelled shutters and the shutter-boxes to house them. In order to increase further the perceived size of the room, we made curtains in a very tailored, precise fashion, hanging them just inside the shutter-box architraves so they are framed by the crisp white outline of the box. This kind of considered, rather architectural curtain-making has a huge impact on small rooms, making the space

A Fez-embroidery covered ottoman of Allegra's design, above, stands in front of the fireplace, over which hangs a George II mirror and drawings by Avigdor Arikha and James Brown. A cabinet, opposite, holds miniature plaster reproductions of the Parthenon frieze, on a base of my design. Over this are pieces by Adam Fuss and Langlands & Bell. The chair is upholstered with one of Allegra's 'Slipping' rugs. The curtains, woven for the room in sand cotton, have a stepped appliqué border in deep pink silk.

103

Our tiny library is comfortable, cosy and filled with our books. The daybeds have thick mattresses covered in Allegra's 'Kali' design, its gold colours echoing the gold weave of the old Sumatran wedding skirt mounted as a blind at the window. The pictures all portray faces, by Donald Baechler, Chris Ofili and Francesco Vezzoli, and a pencil miniature of an admirer of Marie-Antoinette.

seem much larger than it really is; whereas traditional, fussy curtains with fringes, pelmets and tassels, the fabric loosely piling up on the floor in a supposedly 'luxurious' manner, have the opposite effect and shrink a room instantly.

Our favourite room is the new small library. This I designed with a slightly excessive amount of detail, every tiny corner being used, full of secret drawers and panels that open to reveal narrow shelves within. As a family, we live in this room which is unbelievably cosy, like a pre-war railway compartment, and completely lined with books except for corner cupboards holding music and television. The cabinets are designed in a faintly early Renaissance style, with central shelf supports forming slender columns.

Around the top runs a frieze of hand-painted Roman lettering with a coded inscription from me to Allegra. This gives the tiny space a sense of grandeur while also, more prosaically, concealing pipework from the bathroom above. The whole room is painted the same sandy beige as the living room next door. At the single window is a Roman blind made from a striped Sumatran wedding skirt. Two high daybeds, one huge, one small, join together to make comfortable seating for six or even more comfortable lying for two. In front of them, a tall table is perfect for TV dinners for two.

Allegra and I had tremendous rows for the first couple of years over the arrangement of our books, which I insisted be organized by colour. It shocks visitors greatly: they probably imagine them to be 'books by the yard', never opened, never looked at. In fact our little library is our greatest resource and we are constantly foraging through these books for inspiration and ideas. I find that gathering books in coloured blocks makes a room appear much more harmonious and bigger, which in a tiny space like this makes a great difference. Personally I find it much easier to look for a large, red book than to try to remember whether I'd put Athanasius Kircher under Architecture or Alchemy.

For the living room we had settled on a colour scheme of sandy beige walls above a white dado. The chair-rail that separates the two, the skirting and the cornice are all painted in white, or rather just off-white, eggshell or semi-matt oil paint, except for the cornice which is matt like the ceiling. The dado again increases the apparent height of the space and creates a good field for picture-hanging. The floor consists simply of the existing boards, gnarled and marked as they are, painted a slightly off-black colour and covered with one of Allegra's rugs. The other colours are all pinks and reds, introduced in small touches and accents on this beige ground.

While establishing the architecture of the space, we had already planned roughly how to furnish it. This is essential when planning an interior, especially a living room where so much depends on providing enough places for people to sit and ensuring each has a table within reach for drinks, ashtrays and so on. I always draw furnishing plans at a scale of 1:50, which works perfectly. If you cannot draw plans, it is quite practical to make up life-size furniture shapes in newspaper taped together, and move these around the space. So many new houses have unusable space because the architects have failed to consider how they can be furnished.

With its new smaller doors, our living room could accommodate a good, long sofa on the end wall with a table at each end (triangular so as not to block the entrance into the room), a smaller sofa between the doors to stair and library and in front of the chimney an ottoman to provide extra seating that would not block the fire. The triangular end tables were an inspiration which allowed us to have a much longer sofa than we could otherwise have fitted. They are simply cut out of MDF and covered with an Indian embroidered shawl, cut in half to fit both.

The furniture, like the pictures, is a deliberate mixture of old and new, precious and simple. One sofa is absolutely plain, severe and modern, without a curve or a leg

showing, upholstered in plain cotton of a rusty salmon colour. The other is a rather beautiful antique French giltwood affair in Louis XVI style, with a single enormous billowing cushion, covered in a cheap striped cotton weave. On the chimney hangs a George II gilded mirror with old glass; opposite it, an imposing portrait of Edward VII. All the other pictures are drawings by contemporary artists: James Brown, Rosemarie Trockel, Anish Kapoor and Jean-Michel Basquiat (we are constantly asked which of our children drew the Basquiats).

Between the windows we placed a small cabinet containing plaster miniatures of the frieze of the Parthenon, which sits on a base I designed for it. The miniatures are held in leaves of glass and ebonised wood which swing open on silvered hinges to reveal more miniatures within. This makes a very good talking-point and, if stuck for conversation, I always leap up and show off this Victorian curiosity. Above it hangs a wall-piece by sculptors Langlands & Bell, a model of the Pirelli building in gleaming white which works beautifully with the white plaster of the Greek frieze below.

The plain white marble chimneypiece was original to the room, slightly Regency in feeling, elegant but unpretentious. I long to replace it with a beautiful one carved in pink sandstone to my own design, which is waiting in storage until we can afford to pay

for the installation. The gas fire itself was made for us by Tom Dixon, who also made the stair banisters. It is a beautiful, simple piece in steel, which sits on a little canted block of cement that we had made for it.

To light the room, we used table lamps and small, adjustable spotlights in the ceiling. These are placed in such a way that they enhance the architecture rather than intruding on it, with pairs of them centred on each wall and directed at the pictures and objects hanging below them. My father's maxim for lighting rooms – to have as many sources of light as possible but never to see a bulb –

Our bathroom, above, is a small space made more interesting by a sweeping vaulted ceiling, designed to hide exposed pipework from another bath on the floor above. The bath and shower are lined with black 'Vitrolite' glass with silver-leaf edging. On the zebra carpet, a chair by Borek Sipek. The bedroom walls, opposite, are painted to match the natural cotton lining of the bedcurtains, as is the chest at the end of the bed which has tan leather inset panels and straps.

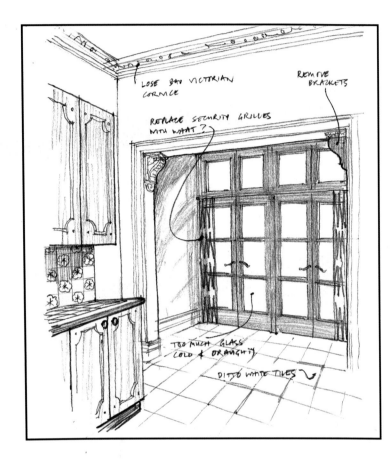

The kitchen before, above, and after our changes, opposite. The windows can be left fully open on those rare warm London days, with the fixed grille outside. The sloping ceiling acts as a vast chimney, with a line of extract fans in the top groove removing all cooking smells. The cabinets and floor are in lightly limed oak with nickel-plated bronze 'Babel' handles. The banquette cushions are covered in Allegra's 'Moon' printed cotton, with my 'Sheaf' dining table.

Perched on sills around the loggia were small glass cases holding models of beautiful country houses, like relics of a lost civilization.

We took the colours for the walls from the old embroidered curtains in dirty pink, terracotta and silver. The 'curtain' pattern came from a piece of nineteenth-century Turkish velvet in the Victoria & Albert Museum. The houses in their vitrines are all Irish, copied from a book which had perfect pictures taken from a helicopter at just the right angle for our room. While the curtains and the glimpses of city beyond are all quite sketchily painted, the houses are minutely detailed, which gives a focus to the space. The cornice, being original to the house, is the only one we retained, scraping off the layers of paint to get back to the raw plaster, which we varnished.

Our own bedroom we made smaller in order to squeeze in a small walk-in closet between it and the bathroom. The room is dominated by a vast bed, bought in the last weeks of Allegra's first pregnancy and so actually much bigger than necessary. To diminish its apparent width, I designed a baldaquin with a corona fixed to the ceiling and curtains hanging from it. This gives the bed so much height that it does seem less wide; it is a dream to sleep in, hugely cosy and welcoming, and besides, our children love to dance on it, swinging on the curtains. The corona is quite small, so the

still holds true, and while we prefer a gentler, less dramatic style of lighting, we always try to keep to this concept.

Our dining room, on the ground floor, is narrow and needed as much extra space as possible. We therefore decided to paint it with a scene that would suggest something bigger. Dining rooms are generally ideal for *trompe l'oeil* effects as they need little furniture around the walls. I came up with the idea of an open loggia atop some giant building, with huge, patterned curtains billowing in a breeze and revealing a view of modern city streets far below.

curtains flare out to create what the French used to call a 'lit a la polonaise'. Unless the room itself is really huge, this always looks more delicate and elegant than the straight-down form of tester bed. Reading lights by a bed are crucial to a happy relationship with both book and partner; ours are modern metal ones with extending arms, on dimmers. Perfect on both counts.

The bathroom had a number of problems, including pipework from above running along one wall, covered by an ugly bulkhead. I designed a vaulted ceiling to conceal the pipes and lend a feeling of space to the small room. Allegra found a zebra-skin carpet that worked beautifully with the black glass edged with silver-leafed wood beading that we had used to line the shower and splashbacks. The washbasin is set in the same black glass with mirrored cupboards on each side. There can never be too much storage space in a bathroom, as every married man soon learns.

We have lived in this house for nine years now, since Angelica's birth, and despite the arrival of Ambrosia, we still fit, if only just. The house grows and changes, moving on with us as we work. There is something hugely satisfying about doing your own house, whether this is also your profession or not. For us, our collaboration started in this house, it is full of joy and memories and it will be a sad day when we have to leave it. But also exciting...

a villa in turin

On the hills across the Po river from the old centre of Turin stand streets of grand *fin-de-siècle* villas and apartment buildings. This project concerns one of the villas, built in 1909 by an engineer without much idea about architecture, but full of the enthusiasm of the time for building something big and imposing. This was a very Beaux-Arts creation, in what is known in Italy as 'Stil Umberto' after their then King. The neighbouring villa, designed by the same man, is almost identical in plan but surprisingly, in a quite different style, adopting a voluptuous Art Nouveau much akin to that of Horta in Brussels, what Italians call 'Stil Liberty'.

Our clients here were an immensely cultured and knowledgeable connoisseur and collector, and her student son. The son was living in Paris, his mother in a beautiful house in Venice. Both wanted to restore life to the villa in Turin, which had belonged to the parents of our client's late husband, and to rejuvenate it. The house had suffered initially from the owners' enthusiasm during the

Fascist years, which resulted in a variety of unfortunate elements (chiefly massive and marble), and later from years of neglect. When we first saw it, it was in a state that would have made Dickens' Miss Havisham feel quite at home.

This was our very first job together; in fact I did most of it, with Allegra contributing some pieces of painted furniture. Some rooms are rather like my father's work, but without his sure hand, and would be done differently today; others I think look good still. When I started on the project we were living in New York where I was working part-time in an architect's office. I drew up the designs in New York and would come out sporadically to meet the client with her very efficient and competent local architect, and view the progress on the job.

The great mistake of the engineer who had designed the house was to give over a huge amount of its volume to the colossally over-sized hall and staircase (see page 92), which left only a relatively little space for reception rooms. There was a large

dining room, but the drawing-room was not only quite small, but also very difficult to furnish, having two windows in one corner, no fireplace and large doors on three of its walls. In retrospect, we should perhaps have adopted a more radical approach and enlarged this room but my client was keen to keep as many as possible of the original features. Since it was my first job I was hardly in a position to speak with great authority.

One of the joys of this job, but also one of its difficulties, was my client's collection of pictures and furniture, exceptional in both quality and sheer size, which meant that there was a lot to fit into

Details from our first commission: an old, wrought iron garden lamp, above, electrified and fitted with a bent copper shade, painted with a Vitruvian scroll motif also used on the walls of the hall; and one of a pair of vitrines, opposite, that I designed to show a collection of miniatures in a small sitting-room. The panelled top holds the fibre-optic lighting system.

The formal dining room, below, in which I made very grand curtains with shaped pelmets to assert themselves over the hopelessly elaborate plasterwork ceiling. The eighteenth-century Venetian chairs are of extraordinary quality. On the walls I hung a collection of Famille Rose porcelain in star patterns reminiscent of seventeenth-century jewel settings. In the more intimate space, right, of the 'office' or pantry, I raised the existing cabinets on slender, tapering legs, giving them new doors with milky opaque glass. Over these I formed panels with painted borders, framing the brackets displaying jewel-like coloured glass pharmacy bottles.

these rooms. I attempted to give some clarity to the design by hanging all the smaller paintings in the drawing-room, reserving a single picture, a truly wonderful, early Madonna and Child, for the new library, while a smaller sitting room had no pictures at all – only numerous mirrors, large and small.

In the same small sitting room, I removed a marvellous collection of miniatures and snuff boxes from a low glass table, where they were always obscured by teacups, books or drinks, and instead arranged them in a specially designed pair of highly architectural vitrines with fibre-optic lighting against a background of darkest blue velvet. The room was dominated by a lovely Della Robbia tondo, and I copied that famous blue for the bands of paper, specially made by Coles of London, that formed panels on the walls to frame the plethora of mirrors. A felt in the same shade of blue was used to cover a pair of Louis XV *fauteuils* with dark wood frames.

The dining room ceiling was a real horror, a rococo-style

plasterwork extravagance painted
dark brown and gold: this I
repainted white with areas of detail
picked out in two different greens.
My client had a wonderful set of
eighteenth-century Venetian chairs
which I upholstered in a red-and-
white striped fabric, together with
elaborate curtains in white with
shaped pelmets bordered in green
in a style sympathetic to the
ornate ceiling. On the walls of this
huge room I hung a beautiful
collection of Chinese Export china,
creating elaborate designs with
them that recalled seventeenth-
century jewellery.

Next to this grand dining room
was a little pantry and breakfast
room, known in Italian as the
'office'. This had another lovely
mosaic floor, with a hexagonal
geometric pattern, partly hidden by
squat cupboards ranged all around,
with solid panelled doors in wood
of a particularly nasty colour. We
kept the cupboards, whose
interiors were perfect, but raised
them on new and simple tapered
legs so that the whole floor was
now visible. Above them, I divided
the walls with painted panels which

framed console brackets to hold a small collection of brightly coloured nineteenth-century glass pharmacy bottles. Allegra added a beautiful painted table-top with a design of Phoenician vases in simulated micro-mosaic.

A lot of my work in this house consisted of cleaning up and stripping out the marble mistakes of the 1940s and some of the excessive paintwork of the original scheme. This was focused on the vast hall, where I painted all the plasterwork a light grey stone colour, removed huge amounts of bad gilding, and introduced my own decorative scheme of huge stars developed from those in the original and beautiful mosaic floor. The woodwork, massive doorcases and skirtings were all in dark polished mahogany and horribly depressing, so these too were painted a stone colour.

In order to restore some of the original decorative paintwork, my client and her architect located a team of expert fresco-painters, who were put to work at once. Inspired by their presence, I started to come up with elaborate painting schemes, such as the stars pattern in the hall and the blockwork in the loggia, described earlier. My personal favourite is the small guest loo (see page 98), which had an existing barrel-vaulted ceiling that we found covered in broken green tiles. For this room I devised an architectural caprice with a Doric frieze, all

The library in the Villa, where I built a room within the walls with tower-like bookcases with obelisk-shaped tapered openings, the insides of which were lacquered midnight blue. I designed the chimneypiece for the room in an aggressively architectural, masculine style of rusticated blockwork to contrast with the delicate, feminine, ethereal painting above it. The low table, featuring two views of Venice, was painted by Allegra in faux micro-mosaic.

executed in a naive 'faux bois', or imitation wood, inspired by some late eighteenth-century Swiss plates I had once seen in Lausanne.

The room to which I devoted most effort was the library, a square room in a corner of the house, where we ripped out the dreary shelving and started afresh. I designed a range of shelves, cabinets and panelling in a severe classical style, stripped of detail and painted in another greyish stone colour. A few open shelves had obelisk-shaped cut-outs lacquered in a glossy midnight blue that set off the glowing brown and gold bindings of the old books. I also designed a heavy chimneypiece, painted a shade darker than the bookcases, playing on the classical architectural motif of rustication. This has recessed, wavy lines echoing the cherubim's wings in the gilded background of the exquisite early Madonna and Child that we hung over it.

A desk of my design, above, with an inset top of tan leather, with an early version of my Klismos chair. The dining room, opposite, painted a faded lilac, leads off the kitchen, the opening **framed by these theatrical curtains. The chairs have hand-painted backs with a motif enlarged from the curtain fabric. The rug was designed by Allegra for the room.**

We were asked by a client to decorate her new apartment, the top two floors of a house in London's Notting Hill. The house had been converted by a developer who had made several bizarre mistakes, including a bedroom that opened on to the living room below, with a constantly leaking tiny roof garden. Our young client (whom I have known since she was four) wanted something that would not look too decorated, would be fun and relaxed but still grown-up enough for her first home.

The whole apartment had been decorated by a previous owner in a rather commercial way, with very elaborate maplewood skirtings, architraves and doors, which gave it the feeling of a hotel suite rather than a home. We kept the doors, which became quite handsome when framed by white painted mouldings. Everything else went, except for the kitchen and bathrooms, which were all good quality and too expensive to change. The priority was to give the living room and bedrooms atmosphere and style.

In Allegra's first conversation with our client, they had found two mutual loves: anything Indian, and the colour lilac. They at once decided on the colours for the small dining room that opened off the kitchen: lilac walls and a new rug, a kilim woven for the room in lilac, off-white and burgundy. A collection of Indian miniatures was framed in cream fabric and hung above a sideboard on the end wall. Curtains in a pretty new version of an old Indian flower motif framed the opening to the kitchen, and also the one window.

The decoration of the living room of the apartment hinges on Allegra's 'Lotus' kilim in a particularly successful colourway of cream, gold, scarlet and blackish purple. Walls are a subtle chartreuse; on them hangs a single picture, a curious Indian watercolour adapted from old maps and town plans, its forms turned into patterns that draw on and link to the other patterns in the space. Below it, a deep and welcoming sofa covered in a traditional Indian print. The other sofa in one of Allegra's modern prints. The chairs, covered in a striped weave, are adapted from the architect Lutyens' favourite chair, ideal for lounging at curious angles. He had adapted his version, in turn, from French Empire 'Meridiennes' that he had seen in an old print of Napoleon. The silver-embroidered cushion has a scaled-down version of the same Turkish carnation pattern that we printed for the curtain fabric, taken from an old velvet bolster. The curtains pull back high up in order to mask the unfortunate height of the window-sills which are up above the exterior building cornice in this third-floor room. On the tables are lamps of Allegra's design, made in hand-forged steel.

The dining chairs came from Habitat, covered in plain off-white cotton on to which our talented friend Mario Penati painted the curtains' flower motif at a much larger scale. These inexpensive but hugely elegant chairs are complemented by a circular table with a floor-length cloth in one of Allegra's first block-printed fabrics, once again in lilac and red. This acts as a permanent cloth over which a plain white cloth is thrown for eating: an excellent formula for dining rooms, which avoids the necessity of buying an expensive dining table that may be the wrong size when you move. Sensible people can put a plastic barrier sheet below the top cloth to preserve the main cloth beneath from stains.

The living room walls were painted in a sagey chartreuse colour, with curtains printed in dark burgundy with a Turkish carnation motif copied from an old velvet discovered at the Musée des Tissus in Lyon. This large-scaled design, which I had drawn, was adapted at a smaller size in silver silk embroidery on magenta cotton to make small cushions, linking the two fabrics in both pattern and colour. I also designed some furniture specially for this room, a pair of curious asymmetrical chairs adapted from a Napoleonic design in the Emperor's library at the palace of Compiegne. These are intended for throwing your leg over the lower arm and warming

yourself by a fire; here there is no fire, but they are very comfortable and amusing to look at.

I also designed a desk for our client, who wanted something practical and pretty. This is painted in one of our favourite stone colours, with an inlaid top of natural leather, and three drawers, one deep for holding files. As a desk chair, we used one of my first Klismos chairs, made at that time by village carpenters in the jewellery shop attic in Jaipur. For this room, another kilim was woven: Allegra's 'Waterlily' design in purple, red and gold on a sandy ground. The modern, stylized flowers of this design are very interesting in juxtaposition with the traditional flowers of the Turkish curtains.

The top-lit stair was extremely dull with light wood banisters and white walls. Allegra printed her 'Tree of Life' design in a golden tobacco colour and had this pasted on to the walls, which gives them a great feeling of warmth and texture. The woodwork was all painted in a dark stone colour and the floor covered in an elegant wool flat-weave carpet, striped in stone, rust and natural, which continued as a runner up the stairs. This awkward space now has enormous atmosphere, especially with the light filtering down from the top landing.

The main bedroom, looking down into the living room, needed to be separated from it at will,

A stair landing, above, with Allegra's 'Tree of Life' fabric stuck to the walls, Roger Oates' striped flatweave carpeting and woodwork painted a dark stone colour. An inlaid Moroccan chair stands under an Indian watercolour Mandala. The bedroom, opposite, has walls in Allegra's 'Trellis' design. The bed has gauzy saris draped from a metal frame and is covered in natural linen with a giant appliquéd Turkish carnation motif.

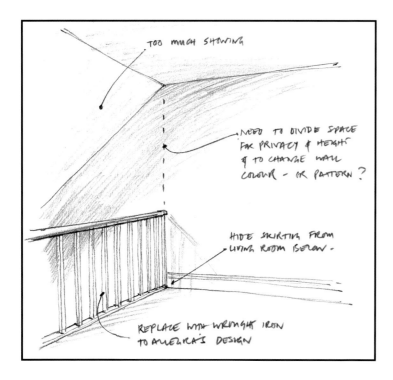

TOO MUCH SHOWING

NEED TO DIVIDE SPACE
FOR PRIVACY & HEIGHT
& TO CHANGE WALL
COLOUR - OR PATTERN ?

HIDE SKIRTING FROM
LIVING ROOM BELOW -

REPLACE WITH WROUGHT IRON
TO ALLEGRA'S DESIGN

The bedroom balcony overlooking the living room, as we found it, above, and now, opposite. The wide sweep of curtains closes off completely when needed. The carnation print appears on the living room side, with a plain red lining to the bedroom. The iron railings have a luxurious handrail covered in suede. The sofa is Allegra's 'Flame' design, covered in plain red velvet. The carpet is wool mimicking sisal, a tan colour shot with red accents that pick up the other reds in the room.

a problem Allegra solved by a theatrical arrangement of curtains tied back around a new wrought-iron balustrade which replaced the boring wooden uprights that had been there. Allegra designed the railing with a free, rambling pattern of branches that was beautifully executed in hand-forged steel, oiled rather than painted or coated so that the metal retained its sparkling, textured surface. On to this went a sensual handrail in natural suede.

The curtains were made in the same Turkish design as those of the living room on that side, and lined with plain burgundy cotton on the bedroom face. As well as separating the two spaces, the curtains cleverly established a dividing line on the wall, so that the surface could change from the chartreuse of the living room to the fabric wall-covering of the bedroom. This was in another of Allegra's first block-printed Indian cottons, in a washed-out Naples yellow with a coral and grey trellis design.

I designed a bed for the room, a romantic thing with a skinny metal frame from which I draped gauzy, transparent ivory saris edged in gold, bought in a famous sari shop in Jaipur. The saris, all five metres long, are cut in half and sewn together lengthwise to make single bed-curtains, then tied on to the metal frame with simple tapes. This gives a relaxed and casual look to this kind of bed, and also makes

it very easy to take them down for cleaning. The headboard and bedspread are in natural linen with an appliquéd design of a huge Turkish carnation motif in purple and grey striped silk. This provides another link back to the decor of the living room below.

The small guest bedroom (see page 89) already had a little alcove formed by cupboards on each side, and in this we placed a bed, covered with old Indian embroideries and patchwork cushions. The walls were painted by Mario Penati with a simplified version of another Turkish flower pattern, this one a stylized tulip from one of those extraordinary appliqué kaftans in the Sultan's personal wardrobe at the Topkapi in Istanbul. The flowers are very much in the spirit of the patchwork cushions and other textiles: in ivory on a ground of spinach green, they have a spare, graphic elegance that transforms this small room.

Five years later, the apartment has grown and developed with its owner, who is now running a small business from it, supplying much-needed and extremely beautiful fairy wings to the young girls of England. The slightly dreamy, romantic atmosphere that Allegra created here, with so many exotic motifs and sources fusing to make one pretty home, finds its perfect foil in the little sparkling gossamer wings that are now being sold from our client's catalogue.

an apartment off eaton square

This client had lived for many years in a small detached house near Eaton Square, where we had decorated several of the rooms separately over a number of years, before she decided to sell the house with its many rooms and buy an apartment nearby with fewer but bigger rooms. Her children had now left home and the old house, with its many bedrooms and floors, no longer made sense, whereas this apartment was perfect for her new lifestyle, which includes a great deal of music, as she is a very active supporter of the London Symphony.

The apartment's last owners had crammed it full of every kind of horror that can be contrived in silk, crushed velvet, gilded plaster and fake marble. Fortunately, our client had the vision to realize that beneath all this vulgarity lay the good bones of handsome rooms that could, without vast expense, be simplified and slightly altered to make a perfect new home for her and her collection of pictures and furniture. We were, however, faced with a number of

unusual problems that presented interesting challenges.

First problem: an entrance hall squeezed, by whoever had converted this huge old house into apartments, below the original stair half-landing. This produced an awkward space with a very low ceiling. Solution: to divide the expanse of ceiling with false beams and mouldings to create a coffered effect that broke it up and gave an impression of height. We also installed spotlights in the floor, shining up the walls, which added still more height. The floor, which had been in two marbles that should never have left Brazil, we laid with glossy black, ebonized boards.

Second problem: making our client's very personal collection seem at home in this quite different new space, which had none of the intimacy of her old, smaller rooms. Solution: to pick one painting from the collection, a small Ben Nicholson abstract, hang it over the fireplace in the huge living room, and use it as inspiration for the whole decorative scheme. In order to

The entrance hall, above, with gleaming ebonised floorboards, natural oak balusters and my 'Sabre' desk. The living room, opposite, has walls painted in imitation of vellum squares, to suit the small scale of our client's pictures, like the Ben Nicholson over the chimneypiece. Either side of this hang eighteenth-century French carved wood panels with musical trophies. On the floor, Allegra's 'Criss-Cross' dhurry.

divide up the vast expanses of wall a little, and to scale them to the smaller works now hung on them, we traced a grid of squares, painted with subtly different shades of parchment by our clever painting team.

The floor, which was in a very expensive dark-coloured parquet, was sanded and polished with a little lime to give it a much lighter feel. On to this went one of Allegra's dhurry collection, in a beige and off-white design perfect for the scheme. For the centre of this big room, as a low table that could double as extra seating when needed, I designed a large X-frame stool with a tan leather seat and dark wood frame. This became part of my Jantar Mantar furniture collection, and has been one of our most successful items.

Third problem: the dining room end of the vast double living room (see page 96), which opened off this entrance hall, with the enormously high ceilings of the original rooms, and a terrible 'alcove' framed by ugly plaster columns of indeterminate style. Solution: to strip out the columns,

creating a new, curved wall framed by a shallow arch in the old alcove, with a lower ceiling to mediate between the two heights of hall and dining room. This made the transition into the great space of the main room easier, while the hall seems less cramped.

The other end of the low entrance hall led to a horrible study with an immensely high ceiling which held a vast cinema-size television in pride of place, and which in turn led to the kitchen. This study became the library and breakfast room, with the ceiling dropped to a good height and well-proportioned bookcases around the three walls without windows (see page 81). A television, music and pantry storage (for glasses, china and so on) went into a wall of closed cupboards. To avoid the monotony of solid doors, I designed this with a breakfront 'temple façade' unit with silver-leaf mirrored doors and sliding shelf units for videos and compact discs.

The lower floor contains bedrooms, arranged around a wonderful internal garden that our

client has made into a fantasy of tall bamboos, a little paradise. The master bedroom was small and lacked a decent bath or dressing room with daylight. These we created by halving the size of another bedroom, making a long space that forms a large, new bathroom and a long dressing area with a window. The bedroom itself gained a small study area with glass doors containing a diagonal trellis pattern of glazing bars that gave it instant style and lightness.

The bathroom, above, seen through a door decorated with applied mouldings. The mirrored doors include backlit panels of opaque glass, the ideal solution to bathroom mirror lighting. The counter and floor are in grey-green Burlington slate. In the bedroom, opposite, we created a new study/ sitting area with delicate glazing in my 'diagonal trellis' design that looks onto the courtyard. The plump armchair and footstool are covered in a printed linen.

a house on lake geneva

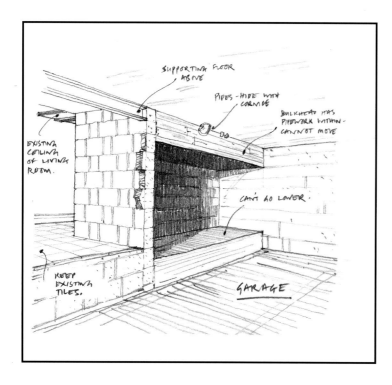

Directoire, with severe, classical motifs in painted wood and other simple materials. These were a great inspiration to us in designing this project, which was intended to have something of their feeling.

The house has been extended over many years from the original small farmhouse and is now a long, straight house with views only towards the lake and small, low-ceilinged rooms. Our clients had started work on a small extension, intending to convert a garage into an addition to their living room. This was the problem that faced us: to incorporate the new space, avoiding the awkwardness that might so easily result.

The garage floor was a metre lower than that of the living room, and its ceiling was also lower. There was a strange alcove in one corner of the ex-garage, with a raised floor slab and a bulkhead above, both of which contained plumbing which could not be removed without excessive cost. This was framed by a supporting wall that could not be removed either. Our client had seen no option for this space but to close it off, using it as

The new living room, as we found it in the early stages of construction, above, and now, right. The major challenge was the dramatic drop in level from the old room down to the new. We solved this by stepping down twice, establishing a moulding that carries the height of the alcove seating area around the space, and using a painted 'mosaic' frieze above.

This old farmhouse overlooking Lake Geneva is the home of a young Swiss family with four children. The house has spectacular views of the lake with Mont Blanc and the Alps looming behind it, an almost unreal picture postcard view. This region has a number of fascinating houses, typically modest and austere Swiss creations, many from the late eighteenth century in a style reminiscent of the French

a ski-store with access from the
end. All in all it was not a promising
start, but there is nothing so
productive as a challenging
problem, and we set to work to
find a solution,

This kind of work is one of my
personal specialities. There are few
things that I enjoy more than a
really awkward space that needs to
be turned into something beautiful.
I worked as an architect for a
number of years after qualifying
from London's Architectural
Association, before shifting the
focus of my work to collaborating
on interiors with Allegra and
developing my furniture collection.
For me, the joy of architectural
work was precisely this kind of
thing: finding solutions to difficult,
problematic spaces, solutions that
would transform every little quirk
and difficulty into a positive
element, so that by the end the
problem would appear to be an
intentional part of the design.

It happened that the entrance
hall of the house had two doors
that almost aligned, one leading
into the dining room and the other
into the existing living room. I took
a line through this second door and
aligned everything with it, forming
a wide, framed opening to the ex-
garage, with steps centred on it,
and a small door beyond into a
new study built on the end of the
garage space. The changes in level
meant that nothing could be done
to put the two spaces of existing
living room and ex-garage together,

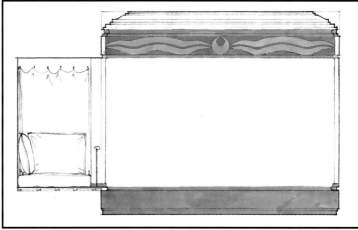

so I resolved to maximize the size and views of the new space and turn the old room into a library with a small sitting area.

The two spaces could be used as one for large parties, while the library would make a cosy sitting room for our clients, alone or with a couple of friends. It is crucial when designing space for other people to obtain an absolutely precise brief, including what sort of entertaining they do and what use they envisage for the various spaces. It is also important to be quite firm in telling clients what is and what is not possible, how many a room will sit, how well a room will work, and what they can and should keep of their beloved possessions. In this case, it was fairly easy, since the clients had already resigned themselves to having two separate small spaces, divided by the new ski-store.

I suggested using the raised alcove space as part of the new living room, making a luxurious

The living room alcove, in my drawing, above, and finished, left, is lined with Allegra's 'Desert Flower' silk, with thick mattresses and cushions covered in a mixture of silks, linens and velvet. The walls are in half-polished *stucco romano* by Giovanni Lombardo, a brilliant local craftsman. The rug is Allegra's 'Sundernagar' kilim.

Details, above, show exotic souvenirs on a sidetable and two sofas with heavy braid trim that invites touch to enjoy their texture, made to our designs by Kingcome. The cushion is reversed: the back of woven fabric is so often more exciting than the front. The library, opposite, was formed from the old, narrow living room, with three walls of books forming a lower, more intimate square around my Jantar Mantar 'X-frame stool'. The existing chimneypiece of local stone was mounted on the face of the new bookcases, with the mirror panel above helping to draw light into this deep space. The two armchairs face another sofa in the window, making a smaller seating group away from the main living room.

high banquette, deep and spacious enough for two people to lie comfortably or three to sit, with low railings matching others framing the steps down from the new library. I had a memory of a Turkish arrangement like this in a yali on the Bosphorus, and it seemed just the thing to give atmosphere and style to this room with its view of the lake. The whole existing ground floor had local terracotta tiles, and we resolved to use these in the new space also.

The new library I designed around the given space and the existing stone chimneypiece, which was brought forward on to the face of the new bookcases. Above it I placed a recessed mirror, with diamond-trellis glazing bars. This motif established a link with the new doors I designed with half-round beadings fixed to the solid flush doors that were required for security and fire safety. The bookcases incorporated a fixed shelf to form a strong horizontal that would continue the line of the new opening to the lower room. Every detail of the scheme was designed to smooth and ease the transition from one space to another, making them seem as far as possible like one large room.

In this way, I broke the line of the step down from the library by pulling it back a little, instead carrying across the lower line of the alcove floor. This continues all round the living room, with narrow, straight colonnettes sitting

on it as a base, and engaging above with a painted frieze that masks the bulkhead over the alcove and also runs all round the room. In this way the entire spatial arrangement, which had promised to be so awkward and ugly, is made to look wholly deliberate, considered and harmonious, and feels totally natural.

Allegra and I then set about decorating the room, using a mixture of her fabrics and others woven specially for it, simple geometric weaves coloured to work with a scheme developed around the terracotta tiles and a pale stone wall colour. We had three new sofas made, all very modern with clean, straight lines, with very tactile braid trimming accentuating their lines. The woodwork was painted in our mid-grey stone colour to emphasize the lines of the new interior architecture, while the alcove was hung with sandy gold silk to give it a real feeling of luxury.

On to the walls, which had been plastered with marble dust to make a lovely sparkling *stucco romano*, we hung a mixture of modern, large Indian watercolours, stylized versions of old pictures, and nineteenth-century landscapes. The finished room is a triumph in that the clients adore it, or at least they tell us so. Certainly it feels happy as a space, is hugely welcoming and relaxing, and has no suggestion of having been such a problem in the beginning.

a house in little venice

The staircase of this typical London house has Allegra's 'Spiral' wallpaper running throughout, uniting the top landing, above, where we hung an antique Indian 'Tree of Life' panel, with the front door, opposite, which is screened from the stairs by a curtain of handloom silk with an embroidered panel of my design. The circular motif on our 'Cintamani' cushions echoes the Regency convex mirror hung on the wall above.

Just north of Paddington Station in London lies Little Venice, a charming area of nineteenth-century canals overlooked by handsome family houses, of which this is one. Our clients were an American family who had recently moved to London, having built themselves a modern house in the States. They were already living in the house, and wanted to do just enough work on it to make it feel more like their own, have a little more style and be a bit less like every other house in London, with expanses of beige carpeting and striped magnolia wallpaper. They also wanted to be out of the house for no more than the length of their children's ten-week school summer holiday.

Allegra and I were very flattered by this commission as they explained that they had been through every interiors magazine they could find, and chosen our work as the only thing they wanted, finding all the alternatives too decorated-looking or too banal. The house required little structural or architectural work, since the spaces were all more or less fixed; this was much more a decorating job, involving stripping out the existing surfaces, altering cupboards and redecorating throughout.

The entrance hall and stair, while wider and better-lit than some, were fairly typical for a medium-sized London house, and badly needed something to lift them and add interest. Allegra designed her first wallpaper for this space, a linear pattern with spiralling hooks which played on traditional striped wallpapers and on imagery recalling Australian Aboriginal drawings. This was printed in soft Naples yellow. Going up through the house, this paper carries the eye from one floor to the next, the hooks creating a rhythm throughout.

Behind the front door and before the stair began was a lobby space which we screened with a fixed curtain of rough silk with an applied panel of some embroidery that I had designed in an odd Graeco-Assyrian style. In this lobby we hung a convex mirror with black edging and a gold frame, above a black cast-iron

bench, the black curves of which echo the lines of the Assyrian 'Tree of Life' in my embroidery. The floor here, and throughout this and the first floor, was in a nasty, commercial-quality light-wood flooring, most unsympathetic stuff which we stripped out and replaced with new, solid oak boards of a good width and ebonized shiny black. This instantly transformed the house.

The living room consisted of two rooms (see page 84) with a very wide opening, which we closed up a little to give it better proportions and also to accommodate bookcases in the smaller of the two rooms, facing onto the canal at the front of the house. We made the simplest of bookcases, painted like the walls, with television and music in closed cupboards beside the chimney. The walls throughout were finished in a *stucco romano* plaster with marble dust, in a faded mustard yellow. We were amazed to find that it cost no more to have the talented Giovanni Lombardo come over from Geneva (where he had already worked for

us) to carry out this work than to use a local contractor.

On to this background of ebony floor and textured yellow walls, Allegra and I now began to place furniture and textiles. She wove a new kilim in her 'Sundernagar' design in a gentle colourway of salmon, scarlet and beige. The curtains for the main living room window, overlooking a generous garden behind the house, were of a natural-colour raw silk, with very wide borders made from an unusual antique red silk *bagh* embroidery that I had found in a treasure trove in Jaipur. We made some clean and simple new sofas, with an assortment of cushions covered in fragments of saris, embroidered

and woven silks in a palette of faded pinks and terracotta.

All of these new things were arranged around our clients' own pieces, such as African masks, antique lamps, a handsome old table with a grey-veined marble top and a pair of Biedermeier stools. They also included a number of beautiful, dream-like photographs by our client, a very talented photographer.

As a centrepiece for the living room, in place of a coffee table, we used one of my new metal X-frame stools with an off-white leather top. In the library end of the room we mounted a magenta-ground *susani*, a chain-stitch embroidered hanging found by our client, as a Roman blind, and

The dining room, opposite, with four of my Sheaf dining chairs grouped around a small antique table. The chairs are loosely modelled on French directoire 1790s period originals; their name stems from the stylized wheatsheaf motifs on the backs, while the shaped cut-outs above (for ease of carrying) are somewhere between an almond and an eye. They stand on one of Allegra's 'Twist' dhurries. The small sitting room (the large one is on page 84) has a single sofa in a heavily textured fabric in a faded rust colour, while two of my 'Thar' armchairs are covered in a hand-embroidered Turkish carnation design that I had done years ago in a sari-embroidery shop in Jaipur.

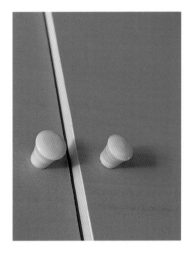

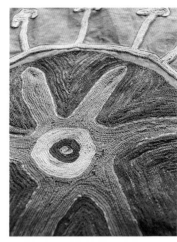

Details of the bedroom, above, show china handles on celadon silk wallpaper, silk crewelwork embroidery and a glass bead fringe on curtains of Allegra's 'Desert Flower' silk. The rug, opposite, is Allegra's 'Fenice' design in lilac, which sits wonderfully with the celadon walls and bedspread, on which is mounted an antique Uzbek *susani* hanging, whose colours have a muted, semi-precious jewel quality. At the foot of the bed stands a beautiful old chest, found by our clients. On the bedside tables are two cheeky Chinese porcelain lamps with shades in our 'Vessel' silk.

we found some old silks in similar colours for cushions on the textured-weave sofa. Our clients also chose a pair of my Thar chairs, which were covered with a silver and magenta embroidery.

Downstairs, we moved the kitchen and dining areas before tackling a conservatory added by previous owners in the large and open rear garden. These conservatories, a feature of so many London houses, are all too often a disaster, being cold in winter, hot in summer and unbearably grey in the sad London light, while the noise of frequent English rain hammering down on their glass roofs hardly bears description. Our solution here was far from radical and changed little but the light, consisting of adding green stained pinoleum blinds to the roof to filter some of the light, and laying Allegra's green 'Twist' dhurry on the floor to warm it. We added dining chairs from my collection, covered in a small green

textural weave, around an antique table belonging to our clients.

The master bedroom has walls hung with a beautiful Chinese silk paper in a pale jade green, which covers cupboards as well as walls. On the floor is a kilim in Allegra's 'Fenice' design, woven for the room in lilac, black and a still paler jade green. The bed is covered with an antique *susani* of great beauty, all sharp greens and pinks, mounted on a soft silk in the same jade as the walls. Curtains for both rooms are in Allegra's silk 'Desert Flower' design, off-white, with a luxurious border of lilac glass beads on a jade green fringe. The whole room has a subtle, quiet, romantic look, very feminine, very appropriate for our client.

The bedroom originally had very little wardrobe space, in the manner of many English houses, where free-standing wardrobes and chests are the tradition rather than built-in closets. We made cupboards to frame the bed, and

Lining the wardrobe doors of the dressing room, which opens off the bedroom, are light, gauzy Punjabi cotton saris in black and cream, right. The sketch below shows the room as we found it, a typically dreary London room with all its elements conspiring to make it seem cramped and ordinary.

stripped out the terrible wall of wardrobe units from the adjacent dressing room. Here we made new units lining the whole of both sides of the room, with doors carefully proportioned to maximize the height and elegance of the space. These consisted of open frames, behind which we hung simple black-and-white woven saris from the Punjab, with delicate little china handles attached.

The new wardrobes frame an existing door on to the landing, with panelled reveals that make it look quite deliberate. The shiny black oak floor, vellum-painted cupboards and off-white saris look simple and hugely sophisticated, while an antique Moroccan rug from the Aladdin's cave of dealer Christopher Gibbs provides the perfect finishing touch. Under the window is an antique French daybed, placed there for our client's highly considerate husband who uses it to read at night without disturbing his sleeping wife: one of those personal idiosyncracies it is vital to discover at an early stage in any job.

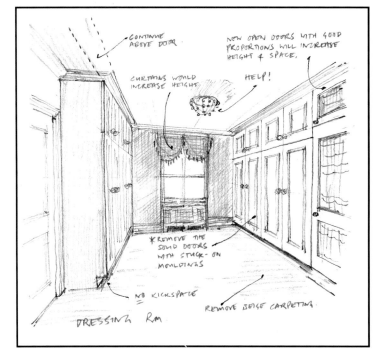

The dressing room, left, seen through the open double doors of the bedroom. The Punjabi saris are hung loosely behind wardrobe doors, but not pleated in that fussy, decorator way. They give a relaxed but luxurious feel to the room, intensely feminine despite the lack of colour. The antique Moroccan rug lies on the same ebonized oak floorboards that we used throughout the house.

141

a house in the country

About an hour from London in the midst of unspoilt countryside, Allegra and I made this house for ourselves out of previously converted old farm buildings when we had only one child. It was the point at which we were just starting to make things, and many of our products and ideas have been tested out here in the country. The buildings themselves are slightly ramshackle, of the typical local construction of brick and chalk. The chalk, cut from nearby pits that still remain, was used only for south-facing walls, but even so it gets very damp.

To simplify construction, the new rooms were built within the old walls, so that they have double-thickness walls nearly a metre thick in places, which gives a wonderful, warm feeling like an old castle. The deep window embrasures are emphasized by angled reveals to admit more light and view, while deep door reveals allow doors to fold back within them and not intrude on the rooms. A great joy of this house for us is that, unlike in London where we tramp up and down stairs all

day, here everything is on one level, except for the children's rooms which are up a tiny stair.

The house is quite small, so I was determined to make as much of the available space as possible, and to waste as little as possible on circulation. A separate little building, an old model dairy from 1820, contains two guest rooms and, with its own separate door from outside, a laundry room. As a result, in the winter months I am not popular with either guests or laundry-users who are all obliged to pick their way across a cold and often rain-swept yard. We do, however, save greatly on space by using the yard as our corridor, however inconvenient it may be.

The main house is consequently devoted almost entirely to rooms, and not to circulation. You enter into a tiny hall, more a lobby, extending to one side with the stair and the door to our bedroom, and to the other opening straight into the living room. The lobby has an internal window facing the front door, giving light into the kitchen beyond, and also a sense of space to the lobby itself,

The front door, above, set in chalk walls and flanked by rustic benches of welded-together horseshoes. The console table surrounded by boots was designed by Allegra, as were the bronze and wood handles, above right, in the living room, opposite. A drawing by James Brown hangs above the fireplace, with a complete Jain horoscope found in Jaisalmer on either side. The chairs are Tom Dixon's 'Baby Fat' and my 'Sheaf Armchair'. On the sofa, Allegra's 'Muskan' print.

I designed this large bookcase-desk, right, for the living room, to have somewhere to work and a place for a few books. With an inset panel of natural leather in the fall-front desk leaf, the front of which has silver-leaf mirror, this is a flexible solution to a very specific furnishing problem. The little pigeon-holes are stuffed with cards, paper and childhood memories, while the simple brackets, above, hold small treasures like a Gallé vase and a Bonnetti-Garouste silver pot filled with sticks of drawing chalk for the children. The chair was my first 'Klismos' prototype.

which would otherwise be claustrophobic. On the window hangs a small picture, a two-sided drawing by James Brown in a glass sandwich frame which allows the back to be seen from the kitchen.

Beneath the window is a console table in wrought iron, designed by Allegra with a leaf motif and a gritstone top which holds every kind of key, gloves, visitors' book and all the rest of the paraphernalia of country weekend life. A large and essential doormat sits on wonderful flat-weave wool carpeting from Roger Oates in a boater stripe, very smart and civilized and surprisingly resistant to country wear and tear. The woodwork, including stair, is painted a light stone colour, while the walls are a deep rust, continued in the kitchen beyond.

The kitchen has an inexpensive wood floor: plastic-coated veneer on board, the kind that comes in packs to lay yourself. This normally looks ghastly but we found that by mixing two colours, laying it in stripes of 'walnut' and 'cherry', you can make it very chic, rather like pre-Renaissance striped stone walls in Siena. The room is dominated by a massive beam of rough oak which replaced the existing central wall and divides the low, flat ceiling in two. The cupboards are very simple, with birch plywood doors and unframed glass panels; the tiles are curious terracotta-on-cream semicircles that we found and that just happened to fit.

I have absolutely no interest in cooking and do nothing in the kitchen except clean up; Allegra, who loves to cook and who makes delicious things (including, I'm happy to say, the world's best chocolate cake), leaves the design and layout of our kitchens to me and is quite happy with the results. I am especially proud of my garbage solution, having seen so many tiny, useless plastic swing-bins in other houses. My version is a 30cm-diameter hole cut in a countertop, with a lid if required, and a full-size plastic bin beneath, in a little cupboard reached from the passage outside the kitchen. It uses up otherwise wasted or impractical corner space, needs changing much less often, and allows you to wipe cuttings and other rubbish straight into it from the counter.

Kitchens are very personal, however, and we tend to leave the design of clients' kitchens to themselves and a specialist kitchen contractor. Between them they always find a solution that works and fits all the clients' individual likes and dislikes, which, in a kitchen, tend to be numerous. For a happy job, we find it is vital to identify areas where the client has a special interest and to look for ways that they can work on this themselves, without our trying to impose alien ideas on them. They hire us to help them achieve a look, not to get the microwave in the right place.

The living room in this house is almost square in plan. Built within

It is, of course, terribly unfashionable to hide your television nowadays, but as long as they remain unsightly black boxes, we don't want to see them. Here our solution was to make a pair of cabinets either side of the fireplace, one for the stereo (and a large collection of LP records that slide out in a vast drawer) and the other for the television and video, below. As the sketch shows, right, the double doors fold back to reveal the entertainment. When closed, they are rather like updated eighteenth-century cabinets, with an old Indian *bagh* embroidery

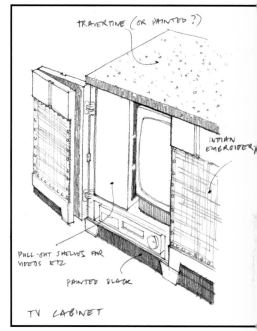

from London's Joss Graham mounted on the front where their noble French antecedents would have had rare Chinese lacquer panels.

USE DEEP CORNICE TO HIDE RAFTER ENDS.

USE BLIND BEHIND CURTAINS TO COVER & INCREASE WINDOW "HEIGHT"

LOSE BEAMS – ROOM TOO SMALL

MINIMISE LOW DOOR – NO ARCHITRAVE.

The sketch, above, shows the problem posed by a small room with a low window, which we solved by cunning curtain detailing, using a fixed Roman blind behind the shaped pelmet to hide the window-head and give an impression of greater height. The curtains are in Allegra's 'Tree of Life'. Two Indian glass paintings hang on the 'green leather' wall.

an old carriage house, it had ugly new timber rafters and beams from a ten-year-old roof that I wanted to hide while retaining as much ceiling height as possible. This we achieved by making a very deep cornice, straight run in fibrous plaster, which emphasizes the symmetrical form of the room and loses the angled rafters above it. The room's pink and green scheme, as described earlier, was inspired by our honeymoon visit to Jaipur, where most of the old city is painted in those colours. The walls here are painted to simulate stitched-together squares of green leather, made by applying differently-tinted varnish on to a base of solid green and stencilling on the 'stitching'.

This curious idea was inspired by a small room in my grandfather's German cousin's last home, Schloss Wolfsgarten, a hunting-lodge outside Darmstadt. This extraordinary house is crammed with every possession and memory of a great German family, including several rooms of products from the famous Artists' Colony of Darmstadt which was built by my grandfather's uncle. The room that I loved best was hung with leather from the hides of deer killed in the park at Kranichstein, another family house, by American bombs at the end of the Second World War. The leather squares were sewn together with large, loose stitches, and hung in the panels of the existing eighteenth-century

panelled walls. It had a simplicity, a roughness, a great chic. Sadly it is now gone.

For one corner of this room, I designed a tall bookcase with a fall-front desk. Closed, the desk part has silver-leafed mirror panels to reflect the room. Open, the flap is lined with natural coloured leather, and the interior has a range of pigeonholes for every kind of memorabilia, writing paper and odds and ends that I find it impossible to throw away. I also made a couple of cabinets for this room to house the television and music. These I made as modern versions of those beautiful eighteenth-century cabinets featuring panels of rare Chinese lacquer or Italian *pietra dura* inserted into a new frame. My version has an old Indian embroidered shawl cut up and nailed into the recessed front, very much less precious and rare than the eighteenth-century models but in the same spirit.

We inserted small windows into the doors of the old carriage house, which we left on the outside in order to disrupt the charm of the old façade as little as possible. This gave us a little low window, which I disguised with curtains and a large, shaped box pelmet, with a fixed Roman blind behind to cover the area of wall over the window head. We worked the same kind of window-trick in our bedroom, at the opposite end of the house in the matching old

A detail, below, of the loose, unlined curtains we made as a relief from the more formal arrangement in the living room. A 1920s French chenille border, found in a market in Paris, provides textural interest while its diamond motifs echo the shape of the windows.

The dining room, right, doubles as studio and when we are in the country we work at this table, made in Turin in 1960. In the foreground stands a pair of chairs made in 1930 in an Alexandria workshop as replicas of Tutankhamun's throne, while the two bookcases were designed by my father in 1965 to hold the albums that they still contain. The floor in local oak was laid by our marvellous local builders, David and Richard Green. The daybed is spread with throws in our 'Herbal' embroidery.

carriage house. There the low window-head is hidden by a huge Roman blind that hangs from the ceiling to just below it, thus implying a much higher window.

Outside the kitchen we added a small dining-room study, approached from the house by a short, book-lined passage. To avoid blocking the daylight from the kitchen windows, and because I love the shape, I made this separate pavilion octagonal. On the outside it has 'rustic columns' in each corner, which are in fact the trunks of fallen trees from the wood next door. This room has three sets of glazed doors with triangular heads in a shape inspired by Grecian doors at the great treasure-house of the Regency aesthete Thomas Hope, The Deepdene. These angles repeat in diamond-shaped windows high on the four remaining walls.

The room has a floor of wonderfully gnarled and knotted English oak, laid in an octagonal shape to follow the outlines of the room. As the curtains elsewhere are quite complicated, and there is never any need to shut out light from this room, we used clip-on hooks from IKEA to hang the simplest, straight panels of printed cotton with 1930s French chenille borders found in a Paris market. A 1960s Italian round table and chairs sit here, the table extended with a loose MDF top and tablecloth when there are more than six to seat. The clean and

In a small guest room, a metal frame over the bed holds a blanket woven in upstate New York in 1823 and decorated with American emblems. On the Maltese chest stands an alarming, early sculpture by Tom Dixon; on the wall behind it a 1753 hunting flag from my German cousins' estate in Hesse.

elegant modern curves of the table and chairs look very happy both with Allegra's voluptuous 'Flame' sofa and with a pair of 1930s reproductions in dark wood of Tutankhamun's throne, bought by my father from an antique shop in Australia.

Of our two guest rooms in the separate dairy, one is a double room with a lot of scarlet silk damask. This was woven specially for my father in 1961, for his vast dining room in the country, a former Catholic chapel with an extravagant domed ceiling

The second room is tiny. It has a single bed with a metal frame holding, as a bed curtain, a beautiful and intriguing American blanket, woven in 1823 in indigo and sandy beige for a certain Sally Ann Drew. As was the fashion of the time, Mrs Drew had the itinerant German weaver incorporate her name along with that of her favourite hero, General Lafayette, and various symbols of the fledgling United States. With this are a 1680s chest of drawers, a couple of 1750s hunting flags, from Schloss Kranichstein in Germany, a frightening-looking head in welded metal made by Tom Dixon in the 1980s, and one of my father's curtain sketches. It all combines to make a very cosy small room, with a host of objects related by colour and texture.

The master bedroom centres on its roman blind of golden silk embroidery, an old *bagh* from the Punjab, set in a border of deep red felt and mounted on new golden yellow *khadi* silk (see pages 72-75). The entire room is built around that embroidery, with golden-yellow painted walls that are wonderfully sunny even on the greyest February morning. Another trick in this room is the insertion of a television into the dressing room beyond, revealed by a small door at table-height. The door is aligned with the top of a little cabinet holding video tapes and the bottom of a picture-frame, so that it is virtually invisible unless open.

Our country bedroom, where every grey English morning looks sunny and bright. The light metal bed frame is draped with Indian handloom silks in wonderful tiger-stripe colours, bordered with Allegra's 'Moon' print. The bedspread is a cintamani embroidered pattern, while the cushions are our 'Emblem' design, inspired by alchemical engravings. The electrician placed the light switches too high here so, rather than move them again at great expense, we hang shell necklaces from them.

featuring the symbols of the Mass in plasterwork. He later re-used the damask for his bed in London, a huge and dramatic creation that formed the focus of his small apartment, standing in the centre of the bedroom which opened — with great double doors always held open — off the living room. Now the damask has been re-used once more, this time to cover the beds in this room, which we painted a dark bronze-grey with white-painted chairs and black and white pictures. The windows have Roman blinds in a strange raffia fabric we found in Venice, woven, we were told, for a couturier but never used.

conclusion

When putting this book together, Allegra and I had no intention of setting out a thesis of some new design style, or a guide to practical decorating hints. We have deliberately avoided recommendations of good colour schemes, formulas for successful rooms or essential rules for furnishing. Instead, we have included a simple selection of our work and some of the inspirations behind it, in the hope that the pictures will speak for themselves.

Design Alchemy began life concentrating on Allegra's rugs and grew until it included product designs from both of us, the inspirations behind them, and our complete interiors that use them. The individual pieces, the inspirations, the various elements that we have combined into those finished interiors, are like the ingredients of an alchemist's work, hence our title which might appear pretentious but is meant most humbly. The alchemy of the reaction to those elements is reflected in our own relationship, a continuation of the male/female principle that lay behind the complex structure of alchemical experiment for so many centuries.

The aim of the book is simply to present some of our work, to explore its roots and its methods, and to celebrate the pleasure that we take in the beautiful things of history and of the present. We would like it to inspire and to inform, just as we have been inspired and informed; we would like to share the pleasure of beauty and, if possible, suggest ideas that others might find useful. In the end it is, like any well thought-out book, a portfolio of things loved by its authors, just as a successful home is essentially a collection of things loved by those who live in it.

bibliography

Inspired by the Classic

The Panorama of the Renaissance
ed by Margaret Aston, Thames &
Hudson, London 1996

The Science of Art by Martin Kemp,
Yale University Press, New Haven
1990

The Red Fort, Delhi by Louise
Nicholson and Francesco Venturi,
Tauris Parke Books, London 1989

*The Golden Calm, an English Lady's
journal in Moghul India* ed by M M
Kaye, Viking, New York 1980

*Flowers Underfoot: Indian Carpets of
the Mughal Era*
by Daniel Walker, Metropolitan
Museum of Art, New York 1997

*The King of the World: The
Padshahnama* by Milo C. Beach,
Thames & Hudson 1997

The Gardens of Mughul India
by Sheila Haywood et al, Thames &
Hudson 1972

*The Architecture of the French
Enlightenment* by Allan Braham,
Thames & Hudson, London 1980

Claude-Nicholas Ledoux 1736-1806
by Anthony Vidler, MIT Press,
Cambridge Mass 1990

L'Architecture de C-N Ledoux,
Princeton University Press 1997

John Soane by David Watkin et al,
Academy Editions, London 1983

Sir John Soane's Museum by Stefan
Buzas, Ernst Wasmuth, Berlin 1994

Pelagio Palagi 1775-1860 by Claudio
Poppi, Electa, Milano 1996

La Villa Kerylos
ed by Régis Vian des Rives, Les
Editions de l'Amateur, Paris 1997

Roman Painting by Roger Ling,
Cambridge University Press,
Cambridge 1991

Ancient Roman Gardens
by Linda Farrer, Sutton Publishing,
Glos UK 1998

Armand Albert Rateau
by Franck Olivier-Vial, Les Editions
de l'Amateur, Paris 1992

*The Decorative Arts in France 1900-
1940* by Yvonne Brunhammer,
Rizzoli, New York 1990

*London Interiors from the Archives of
Country Life* by John Cornforth,
Aurum Press 2000

David Hicks on Decoration-5
by David Hicks, Britwell Books
London 1972

David Hicks on Living with Design
by David Hicks, Weidenfeld &
Nicholson London 1979

Jean-Michel Frank
by Leopoldo Diego Sanchez,
Editions du Regard, Paris 1997

Les Decorateurs des Années 40
by Bruno Foucart, Norma Editions,
Paris 1998

Design Evolution

Patterns that Connect (Tribal Design)
by Carl Schuster, Abrams,
New York 1996

Costumes and Textiles of Royal India
by Ritu Kumar, Christie's Books,
London 1999

*The Kashmir Shawl and its
Indo-French Influence*
by Frank Ames, Antique Collectors'
Club, Suffolk UK 1997

Silks for the Sultans
ed by Ahmet Ertug, Ertug and
Kocabiyik, Istanbul 1996

Jewelry from Antiquity to the Present
by Clare Phillips,
Thames & Hudson 1996

*The Furniture of the Greeks, Etruscans
and Romans* by G M A Richter,
Phaidon, London 1966 (1st ed
Clarendon Press Oxford 1926)

Furniture, The Western Tradition
by John Morley, Thames & Hudson,
London 1999

Le Mobilier Francais: Les Sieges
by Guillaume Janneau, Les Editions
de l'Amateur, Paris 1989

Primitivism in 20th Century Art
ed by William Rubin, Museum of
Modern Art, New York 1984

General

The House of Life by Mario Praz,
Methuen, London 1964

*An Illustrated History of Interior
Decoration from Pompeii to Art
Nouveau* by Mario Praz, Thames &
Hudson 1982 (1st ed 1964)

*Authentic Décor: the Domestic Interior
1620-1920* by Peter Thornton,
Weidenfeld & Nicholson 1984

*Twentieth Century Decoration: the
Domestic Interior*
by Stephen Calloway, Weidenfeld &
Nicholson 1988

Billy Baldwin Decorates
by Billy Baldwin, Chartwell Books,
New Jersey 1972

*The Golden Game,
Alchemical Engravings*
by Stanislas Klossowski de Rola,
Thames & Hudson, London 1988

*The Hermetic Museum: Alchemy &
Mysticism* by Alexander Roob,
Taschen, Cologne 1997

useful addresses

Boutique for our home accessories
and Allegra's fashion collections:
Allegra Hicks
4 Cale Street
Chelsea Green
London
SW3 3QU
Tel: 020 7589 2323

Showroom for Ashley's furniture, open
to trade and retail customers alike:
Jantar Mantar Showroom
2/27 Chelsea Harbour Design Centre
London
SW10 0XE
Tel: 020 7351 2223
http://www.jantarfurniture.com

For Allegra Hicks rug collections in
kilim and hand-knotted wool qualities:
Christopher Farr
212 Westbourne Grove
London
W11 2RH
Tel: 020 7792 5761
http://www.cfarr.co.uk

For bespoke/custom rugs, the Dhurry
Collection and our fabric collections:
Allegra Hicks Showroom
2/27 Chelsea Harbour Design Centre
London
SW10 0XE
Tel: 020 7351 9696
http://www.allegrahicks.com

Full details on Allegra Hicks and
Jantar Mantar representation in
the USA and elsewhere can be
obtained from the showrooms
or our websites.

For Allegra's wallpapers and David
Oliver's beautiful paints:
Paint Library
5 Elystan Street
London
SW3 3NT
Tel: 020 7823 7755
http://www.paintlibrary.co.uk

The upholstery throughout this book
was mostly made by:
Drapes Design Co
40-42 Couching Street
Watlington
OX9 5QQ
Tel: 01491 612291
http://www.drapes.co.uk

Makers of the best sofas we know,
including many of those illustrated:
Kingcome Sofas Ltd
1/12 Chelsea Harbour Design Centre
London
SW10 0XE
Tel: 020 7352 1005

Stucco Romano by Giovanni
Lombardo, available through
Allegra Hicks Showroom
Tel: 020 7351 9696

Finally, four treasure troves of
antiques, accessories and textiles:
Christopher Gibbs Ltd
3 Dove Walk
Pimlico Road
London
SW1W 8PH
Tel: 020 7730 8200
http://www.christophergibbs.com

Joss Graham Oriental Textiles
10 Eccleston Street
London
SW1W 9LT
Tel: 020 7730 4370

La Joya
24 Cheval Place
London
SW7 1ER
Tel: 020 7823 8066

Themes & Variations
231 Westbourne Grove
London
W11 2SE
Tel: 020 7727 5531

Museums
Sir John Soane's Museum
13 Lincoln's Inn Fields
London
WC2A 3BP
Tel: 020 7405 2107
www.soane.org

Pitt Rivers Museum
School of Anthropology and
Museum Ethnography
South Parks Road
Oxford
OX1 3PP
Tel: 01865 270927
http://units.ox.ac.uk/
departments/prm

Musée Carnavalet
23, rue de Sévigné
75003 Paris
Tel: +33 1 42722113

Musée des Arts Décoratifs
Palais du Louvre
107 rue de Rivoli
75001 Paris
Tel: +33 1 44555750
http://www.ucad.fr

Musée des Tissus
34 rue de la Charité
F-69002 Lyon
Tel: + 33 4 78384200
www.lyon.cci.fr/musee-des-tissus

Villa Kerylos
Impasse Eiffel 06310
Beaulieu sur Mer, AM
Tel: +33 4 93016170
www.villa-kerylos.com

Scuola di S. Giorgio degli Schiavoni
3259/a Calle dei Furlani
Castello
Venezia, Italia
Tel: +39 041 5228828

Pelagio Palagi Collection
Museo Civico Archeologico
di Bologna
Via dell'Archiginnasio 2
40124 Bologna, Italia
Tel: +39 051 233849
www.comune.bologna.it/
bologna/Musei

Castello di Racconigi
Via Morosini 1
Racconigi, Italia
Tel: +39 0172 84005

index

index

acknowledgments

picture credits

Conran Octopus would like to thank the following photographers and organizations for their kind permission to reproduce the photographs in this book.

Acknowledgements in Page Order

4-5 Christopher Farr (Designer: Allegra Hicks); 12 National Archeological Museum; 13 Richard Bryant/Arcaid/96; 14 KEA/Francesco Venturi; 15 main picture Museo Thyssen Bornemisza, Madrid; 16 Scuola di San Giorgio degli Sciavoni, Venice/Bridgeman Art Library; 17 Metropolitan Museum of Art, Rogers Fund 1939; 18-19 KEA/Francesco Venturi; 20 Phototheque des Musees de la Ville de Paris/Abdourahim; 20-21 RIBA Library Photographs Collection 21 Bridgeman Art Library (Giraudon); 22 Richard Bryant/ Arcaid; 23 above Richard Bryant/ Arcaid; 23 below by courtesy of the Trustees of Sir John Soane's Museum; 24 Bibliotheca dell' Archiginassio, Bologna; 24-25 Tim Imrie/Country Life Picture Library; 25 above right Bibliotheca dell' Archiginassio, Bologna; 26-27 Martin Scott; 27 Martin Scott; 28 Scala; 30 Musee des Arts Decoratifs/Laurent-Sully Jaulmes; 31 Musee des Arts Decoratifs/Laurent-Sully Jaulmes; 32-33 Country Life Picture Library; 40 Simon Brown/The Interior Archive (Property:Pitt Rivers Museum); 41 The National Gallery, London; 42-43 Christopher Farr; 43 Universitatsbibliothek, Heidelberg; 44 above Brigitte Thomas/The Garden Picture Library; 46 Staatliche Museen zu Berlin/Bildarchiv Preussischer Kulturbesitz Gemaldegalerie (Photo: Jorg P.Anders 2000); 47 below left Tate Gallery, London (Fondazione Lucio Fontana, Milan); 48 above right Steve Allen/The Image Bank; 51 above right V & A Picture Library; 52 above right and below Topkapi Museum, Istanbul; 55 above right British Museum; 55 below right Staatliche Museen zu Berlin/Bildarchiv Preussischer Kulturbesitz Antikensammlung (Photo: Ingrid Geske 2000); 56 above left and right National Archeological Museum, Athens; 56 below left AKG London/Erich Lessing; 59 centre right Musee des Arts Decoratifs, Paris/Laurent-Sully Jaulmes; 60 left Werner Forman Archive/British Museum, London; 61 right Photo RMN/Franck Raux; 63 main picture AKG, London/ Erich Lessing

acknowledgments

author's acknowledgments

We would like to thank, first and foremost, our ever-indulgent clients, who had the patience and kindness to allow their homes to be photographed again. They asked to remain nameless and so they shall.

We should also thank everyone who has helped us to create not only what is shown in this book but everything since, especially Tania Martin and Perdita Roschker; Mani Mann and her team; Munnu Kasliwal; Christopher Farr and Matthew Bourne; Micky Shane, Henry Millington and Samiir Wheaton.

First published in 2002 by
Conran Octopus Limited
a part of Octopus Publishing Group
2-4 Heron Quays
London E14 4JP
www.conran-octopus.co.uk

Text copyright © Ashley Hicks 2002
Book design and layout copyright ©
Conran Octopus 2002
Photography copyright © Ashley
and Allegra Hicks 2002

Publishing Director: Lorraine Dickey
Senior Editors: Emma Clegg and
Gillian Haslam

Creative Director: Leslie Harrington
Creative Manager: Lucy Gowans
Art Editor & Director of Special
Photography: Karen Bowen
Special Photography: Bill Batten
Picture Research: Sarah Hopper

Production Manager: Adam Smith
Senior Production Controller:
Manjit Sihra

British Library Cataloguing-in-Publication Data
A catalogue record for this book is available from the British Library

ISBN 1 84091 193 X

Printed and bound in China